Le Femme

and the Communist Spirit

Written and Illustrated by
Karen Kellock Ph.D.

A complete theory based on Einstein physics,
Political Psychology, Systems Theory
and Archetypal Psychiatry.

FORMULA
All success attraction
All disease obstruction
All recovery elimination

You must fast on all three
OBSTRUCTIONS:
People
Habit
Food

Le Femme

FEMME

FRENEMY

HIPPY

COMMIE

AUTOPHAGY

LADY

LE FEMME

"I'm not angry I just have a hot temper and I'm passionate about certain things" she shrieked.   Women aren't born dumb they adapt to other women. Female culture is a massive impediment to genius. Those who break through are rare variations for the commie spirit wants open borders, approval of others, big government. Nothing's more wrong than a liberal feminist and to think we had to adapt to that as kids! Races help each other up, so too religions and men do--but women push each other down, cruel.   Get Jezebel outa your life or she'll ruin it with strife.

Written and Illustrated by
Karen Kellock Ph.D.

Femme

There were several Jezebels I had to contend with,
the scariest of all eras and most destabilizing.

 "I'm not angry I just have a hot temper and I'm passionate about certain things" she shrieked.

Women aren't born dumb they adapt to other women.

Female culture is a massive impediment to genius. Those who break through are rare variations.

Le Femme and the Communist Spirit: Wants open borders, approval of others, big government.

Nothing's more wrong than a liberal feminist and to think we had to adapt to that frustration as kids!

Races help each other up, so too religions and men do. But women push each other down, cruel.

What a sorry sight to see one so blind to their deficiencies and deep in denial: Hillary. Nigel Farage

Get Jezebel outa your life or she'll ruin it with strife.

It's been proven for decades in serious bully studies that female bulls are social/many friends

LE FEMME and the Communist Spirit

Nothing's worse than a tyrannical harridan in the home with wimpy hubby acting like a silly pawn.

Female bullying is most vicious, taking the form of reputation destruction, innuendo and gossip.

Girls who bully have many friends, are socially skilled and act in groups: destroy reps/spread the scoop.

Feminists: a genuine rape culture is spreading across Europe not a made-up one like yours.

Feminists complain about mansplaining or leg-spreading while Europe is conquered thru gang-raping.

The feminists hating males cuz they're a western man but then loving Jihadis, unbelievable.

The man-hating feminist wants to be crushed. She wants to be shoved around a little after all this.

"To keep em under control was not difficult--fill up their time/minds." Orwell

Consequence-free virtue signaling: a fundamentalist of feels.

Their virtue signaling is totalitarian: you dam well tow this line or we will call you unforgiving.

All you can do is stay away and if you do you'll be ok.

God gave me success when I learned to treat my husband right. Joyce Meyers

Have a fifties lifestyle no matter what's going on: lock the gate and concentrate on those at home.

LE FEMME and the Communist Spirit

What does it mean to be loved by a woman--does it mean to be broken so her vanity's not threatened?

Men are only mean when you act that way. In relationships be normal and decent and all is ok.

You can't trust women anymore guys--find one who didn't go to college.

Jezebel floozy: don't trust her just cuz the dogs and cats love her.

You thought she was stunning 'til you found out she was nothing and what a shock honey.

Education is destroying the soul. A Ph.D. with no common sense at all.

Having two liberal sisters/social mother I know all about women and like the plague avoid em.

Men are weak cuz their dads were gone, brought up by mom--its her anger when they speak.

Mom and two feminist sisters were illogical as Merkel and I often cried from the contradictions, hysterical.

You're not a misogynist cuz you're telling the truth about what women are doing.

If left approves cuz you reinforce their weirdness they'll love you but you're going to hell miss.

If they want you nothing will keep em away but if they don't want you nothing will make em stay.

Patriarchy plus chivalry equals happy women and societies.

LE FEMME and the Communist Spirit

Sweeter they are the more virtue signaling but God wants us bold/strong not such obvious faking.

The most insecure women brag of their strength more. "I'm a strong woman--hear me roar"

In a post-Christian era female goddess religions emerge and lesbians become preachers.

Women's studies and ethnic studies are pseudo-disciplines and degrading quality of the real ones.

JEZEBEL SPIRIT

Jezebel can't help doing what she does, that spirit compels her to be a disgusting scuzz.

It's a spirit: Jezebel doesn't realize she's stealing, grabbing, dividing and manipulating.

Jezebel can't help saying crude things, it's spirit in her but you still must cut her loose to be king.

Jezebel can't help her grabby behavior it's weakness allowing that spirit/need the Savior.

Jezebel can't help what she does under spirit's influence but get strong so she's not a nuisance.

Jezebel spirit only gets worse until you stand against this curse coming thru women even a nurse.

Jezebel takes, meddles, gossips, divides/grabs but I want a humble maid just doing what I ask.

LE FEMME and the Communist Spirit

No logic with Jezebel. She's slippery changing the subject five times a minute so you won't know.

Since she can't be pinned down confusion keeps her on the throne so remove her then be known.

Jezebel has a secret agenda always and lies convincingly for praise and the confusion is a haze.

You can't reason with her, she never *ever* admits fault and she doesn't learn-- she's not the salt.

Even the most absurd things she obviously did she won't admit to, it's a prideful spirit too.

We've all known a Jezebel that changed our lives forever when we finally let it go/got clever.

The Jezebel seemingly rips from you your right to choose and man she really brings the blues.

Women: For you to forgive without repentance is creating a monster with you the dunce.

Jezebel gets your emotions stirred up then lets you go into a rage like she's the innocent sage.

Jezebel spirit will make you think you want her, it's actually a gut feeling of terror mislabeled in error.

The Jezebel spirit in the house from the maid made me crazy, sorry, but now it's explained.

Jezebel spirit was dormant until feminism triggered the varmint/now we're all suffering with it.

LE FEMME and the Communist Spirit

Those influenced by a Jezebel spirit always target a leader. They want all the attention and power.

The Jezebel spirit is always the victim and wants your pity. Mom makes you hate dad, shut up lady.

Maxine Waters is the Jezebel of the Hour.

When Jezebel is humble it's a religious spirit and just more trouble.

Jezebel is a self-important heretic even calling herself a "prophetess"

Simply put, Jezebel is a divider, a slighter and a Queen Bee dominator/you'll only rule without her.

Jezebel will insidiously worm into your household and you'll even love her cuz the spirit's so bold.

Jezebel is never wrong, it's always "them". Just to get on your good side she'll seemingly repent.

Don't make the Jezebel housekeeper part of your family or you'll be in divorce court speedily.

Jezebel is *never* accountable and if you ever confront she'll cry and accuse/call you a Jezebel.

Jezebel spirit looks for the hurt, wounded or insecure to become their spiritual guide/teacher.

Just when you think she's repentant an opportunity arises and she creates another terrible crisis.

Jezebel is so insidious you must eliminate the influence--don't let her back in to stay a Mrs.

LE FEMME and the Communist Spirit

 Jezebel comes thru men too but a power trip comes from early rejection more often with women.

Jezebels guilt-trip calling you unChristian for not bowing to their needs--don't feel guilty, please!

Best housekeepers are invisible, humble, silent and never take sides if they want employment.

Once out, you can knock all you want broad you'll never get back in cuz we see your facade.

Jezebel twists facts/has selective memory. She's smooth, slick and convincing as her armory.

Even a court of law can't pin Jezebel down.

Jezebel wants what you have and prays "remove that person--that position belongs to me."

When you see Jezebel in your midst you must nip it in the bud or the damage will quickly erupt.

The Jezebel spirit will act in ways causing great suffering and damage along the way. Fire, today.

It isn't just your tragedy. Check out what feminists have done to you, your world and family.

Men used to love women/would never hurt em--but feminism has made em a terrible burden.

Women don't want men getting together and discussing without them there as controllers.

All liberal women hate men. Jesse Lee Peterson

LE FEMME and the Communist Spirit

They leave for college as sweet little girls and come back raving lunatics influenced by that world.

If the pastor preaches on the Jezebel spirit to scare then that spirit sure won't want to stay there.

Reactive Illness: several wives of Jezebel husbands died in their forties after abuse/suffering it.

The Jezebel spirit has claws and charisma as it gains tragic hold and attaches to intelligentsia.

In an effort to gain an indomitable footing the Jezebel spirit will attach to someone good looking.

News outlets are not about reporting news but controlling and shaping reality.

NYC will regret an evil nasty woman won, a socialist handing out free stuff. Jesse Lee Peterson

Jezebel also causes water retention. We bloat with vile insubordination esp. when paying em.

If a Jezebel Spirit's in your life you'll do absurd things and have weird dreams at night.

Your gut is terrified of this woman but magically reverses to attraction so watch out/take action.

Why are women so terrifying? It's a God-given body they're defiling and things they believe in.

Just from things they say you know they're crazy, mimicking common narrative like all mentally lazy.

LE FEMME and the Communist Spirit

It's the sweet little old ladies who are filled with heresies and will ruin your life taking their advice.

It's a bottomless pit, a dark infinite cavern--that's the godless woman and I know you've met one.

They can't help what they say, it just all pours out: the filthy cesspit of the nasty women faking clout.

She'll do anything, a nasty woman without lines. She'll turn on you too, infidelity of the unkind.

She's unstable, her moods variable. You can't trust her, the untrustworthy and unreliable.

The nasty woman goes to greatest lengths to be as nasty, filthy and disrespectful as she can be.

New women take pride in being nasty/dirty even calling themselves sex pots and having parties.

Women are the problem making anti-family/men decisions and Obama got in because of them.

Women are incapable of seeing the outcome of their lousy decisions/repeat path of destruction.

Women make decisions by how they think/feel, men make em on logic and seeing the outcome.

Men tolerate the feminist BS from a desire to be fair and have tranquility and peace at any price.

Women-hating men aren't born that way. It's adaptation to angry mama or girlfriend along the way.

LE FEMME and the Communist Spirit

Poor men are ruined by divorce: they can't see their children but still must pay child support.

Men gossip but women are ruthless/tireless. It's their whole thing, it makes their day/hell to pay.

It's true, women's scorn is worst than men's. It's due to their tenacity in getting back/irreverence.

Every woman has been lashed by a female enemy. They're assiduous, won't give up, oh my.

Danger of female enemies is their major weapon: ruthless gossip, but God hates this. Prov. 20:19

NO feminist woman is sweet, loving, tender or nurturing. Man, they believe in baby killing!

I was targeted by a feminist using gossip/unfair and felt like a cat in a room full of rocking chairs.

It was a small desert town and she managed to turn every one against me then I awoke/could see.

I was a recluse, not social. She was ultra-social, being liberal. She had the edge, I was the fool.

I'd gladly give up the vote to cut dangerous women outa politics completely, that's no joke.

Women are ruining men and children for life. With men gone world seems dark/filled with strife.

Divorce brings down a home (more than house) and the pets go to the shelter. It's so sad, a killer.

LE FEMME and the Communist Spirit

Even long term successful marriages are ended by women for the hell of it, and it's his end.

Any divorce is as terrible as it gets. Everyone suffers especially the kids and pets.

Feminism is immoral.

New women don't want men getting together without them sitting there controlling male behavior.

My experience of men is they'll do anything to keep me happy, but liberal feminists are crazy.

What made me an anti-feminist was run-ins with narcissistic women feeling blasphemed or dissed.

Feminism is ruining families and it need not be, things are beautiful if (of this falsity) we're free.

You see tiny children flipping the bird and using F-Talk, all from mama's encouragement, yuk!

All her decisions are wrong, not based on logic but false theory, feelings, empathy, virtue signaling.

They presuppose the impermanency of marriage. It's always on probation and not a good ending.

They put Johnny in therapy for wrong reasons only to be brainwashed by new age heretic legions.

A maid even tried to divide us, everyone's a feminist by default even if they think they're not.

LE FEMME and the Communist Spirit

Jezebel is so very clever she'll worm in and stay forever then you'll even say "oh well, whatever".

Wimps: The man can't do what he wants but she can do whatever she wants when she wants.

Smart women take the side of men and hate feminism.

Feminists take pride in being sluts or anything else they want. Saints have restraint/are loved.

Germany ruined by a woman. They weren't born dumb but made that way like with Mrs. Macron.

Penetrate network and your head fills up with cobwebs of "who said what to who"/screwed.

They mistake virtue signaling with virtue by taking a stand on something that is moral in nature.

Taking a moral stand they become obdurately immovable and fixed--it's women doing this.

They lecture you on false ethics and can't shut their mouth about it.

Women are the worst with false ethics when they make it politics.

Biggest contradiction in your life: girlfriend sympathizes with destructive people filled with strife.

Stop being misadvised by false Christians who are pagans and see virtue signaling as goodness.

These women are just trying to look good/have a nice image. This they call politics but it all sux.

LE FEMME and the Communist Spirit

Be a model of niceness and a nice life for those who've devolved to clutter, chaos and strife.

Fake feminists can live with contradiction because that's what they are already so I'd avoid em.

Women: vapid platitudes/childish naiveté seen as the only reality and making sure you agree.

Germany debates putting troops on streets against ISIS. This is moving fast, a female induced crisis.

Of course not all women are insane, it's a bell shaped curve. We're the edges but movin' in to serve.

The vacuity in most women is a mix of feminism, pathological altruism and not knowing anythin'

Western women are poisoned by generations of feminism.

Where women rule, feelings/emotions dominate the political landscape not reason and logic.

Weird feminist creed: Be tolerant of the intolerant.

Whatever he did to Mary his karma was Sue and now he's got me since he's paid his dues.

After rejecting patriarchy white women want meaner men and are wearing hijabs everywhere today.

Women going along with modern feminism are then pimped by it. Alex Jones

LE FEMME and the Communist Spirit

Feminists who've battled husbands or ruined them in divorce have fallen for Jihadis of course.

Omarosa: We all know a person who will turn on you cannot be trusted. Traitors are hated by both sides, busted.

Women aren't held back by men as feminists suggest. It's not patriarchy it's brain mass.

They disparage/trash women of substance while they laud a porn queen: that's the liberal scene.

Girly men aren't innocent if they gossip like a girl so don't trust em, male feminists are sadists.

Don't believe what mom says about dad or what he says about her. Go to that person, hear?

Don't listen to mom about dad cuz that's her feelings not yours, judge for yourself after divorce.

Don't listen to mom/dad about your crazy uncle/aunt either. Genius/saints are hated tho' clever.

If mom/dad are liberal they hate conservative aunt/uncle so make your own decisions if able.

Was your aunt hated as a conservative or sinner? For you could have learned stuff from her.

God is within so everything you're looking for is already there, but you forgot distracted by glare.

He never beat her up nor had an affair. But to hear her talk you'd think he was a sadist I declare.

LE FEMME and the Communist Spirit

Mother wasn't a raving harridan but submissive and sweet, looked much better/able to think.

How funny: Angry, fat, ugly feminists saying men are raping em when all they want is to escape em.

Vindictive women taking advantage of the social climate and pinning men with things/ruining them.

Women love girlie men (more controllable) and that's why they loved Obama despite being a dictator.

Barrack Obama was a feminist and look what happened to the country: he almost finished it.

Trump is the forgotten man from the fifties core--that's why we love him: we don't have it anymore.

They loved the girlie man (fake tears) Obama who tried to destroy the country of America.

The perfect Order of God: God in Christ, Christ in man, man over woman, woman over children.

Barbaric terrorist refugees are hot items with Swedish gals after their men became cucks and fell.

Problem is the women's vote. They took men way, gov. is husband--that's all they want.

Women are spoiled by spineless girlie men so go wild with anger/regression with the real man.

They aren't used to real man, calling em animals--they've been spoiled by girlie men they know.

LE FEMME and the Communist Spirit

Men are to be head of their wives (not "household"). But even preachers are afraid to be bold.

Even strong men are terrified of their wives saying "God rules her" rather than "I rule"/terror.

Even preachers are controlled by wives (tho' they play a role)--not children of God as foretold.

I have never met such pansies: men terrified of women. It's sickening not just wimpy/we hate em.

Men are to rule women but modernity makes that thought a trigger of contention with woman.

If he rules her she'll get all her friends against him then they gossip/mis-advise to get rid of him.

Men: If you don't man-up they'll take the manhood out of you for good.

Absent fathers/brought up by liberal mothers = catastrophe: girlie men or women who are angry.

Black preachers supporting everything wrong: controlling wives and Black Lives Matter/strife.

Feminists use rejection/discord as a rudder to control systems and they pass this onto sons.

Feminists/liberals hate white, straight, hetero Christian males who are becoming girlie, cucked, frail.

When feminism gets in a woman's system she starts bitchin'

LE FEMME and the Communist Spirit

Marrying a prince is marrying into patriarchy. It's amazing any "feminist" would do that, malarkey.

Feminists hating men are going crazy over Trump cuz he's the epitome of what a great man is, luv'.

As he plowed thru the vicious crowd trying to kill em she said "aren't you gonna try to *help* him?"

Women have it so badly turned around it's a wonder we're still here after they got vote/took over.

If you don't know principals (property) you vote BIG GOV and socialism via virtue signaling.

Would feminists ever admit gender inequality doesn't exist? No cuz it doesn't suit their interests.

Moreover, look at the poor women in other countries then tell me your troubles honey.

Not only do women control men thru sex, they ruin the lives of their ex.

When women control men thru sex it's not sexism, but when men do it it is? This is typical bias.

What does feminist Meghan say about the spiking of female genital mutilation in the UK?

Feminist in name only: I'm all for equality but I'm marrying into royalty.

Me Too: all jumping on bandwagon saying they were raped--watch for false charges and escape.

LE FEMME and the Communist Spirit

Advised by a shady liberal feminist to divorce she ruined and devastated her life of course.

She/he's trying to tell you white is black and you're going along with it?

Women are idiots when it comes to politics. Open borders, gov. tyranny–these are facts, look at stats.

If women don't know principals they succumb to shallow surface emotionality, prey to drama.

Worldwide, women know less about politics than men and aren't up with current affairs, just friends.

Regardless of "gender equality" women know less than men about politics, it's just a fact.

Women repeatedly vote against own interests and don't know it, virtue signalers easily molded.

The more privileges a woman has the less she knows about politics. Less gender gap = social/gossip.

The more "equality" she gets the less she knows about politics--I just can't get over that.

You'd think increased female presence in politics would bring kindness not killing and ruthlessness.

In high IQ areas there are only men, not women--these female deficiencies are blamed on men.

It's a huge problem: the more power women get the less they know.

LE FEMME and the Communist Spirit

Women are so vastly uninformed yet arrogant about their opinions since it's all virtue signaling.

Women are significantly uninformed compared to men and thus female genius has no friends.

Scary: women are voting but are FAR less informed than men (see stats friends),

Women are less informed and vote left. Test me on this: sit down and talk with her about politics.

People are surprised I would take men's side--that's a sign identity is all and logic is gone.

Some women are logical--those who break thru become the best: smart, spiritual and practical.

Their answer like reflex: The problem is not that women are uninformed but that men are sexist.

A pernicious lie: "Men privileged, women oppressed. Hire, promote and reward accordingly".

Do not give women power over sexuality. Stefan Molyneux

Never pay her bills cuz she's sleeping with you--that's paying for sex and devalues her too.

Never date a woman if she's trashy, empty, shallow or useless. Just turn away, no need to address.

Science shows women feel far more pain than men so don't send em to war if you're their friend.

LE FEMME and the Communist Spirit

Women vote for bigger government esp. single moms, they see it as security and protection.

Married women go conservative since they don't want state to take the stuff the husband built up.

Creeping socialism in the west, massive emotionality, uninformed women on a worldwide scale.

In Sweden, voicing an opinion saying there are men vs. women can truly bring you opprobrium.

Destroying gender roles is the major way they weaken society along with the migrant tsunami.

She may be smart but what she needs is education of the heart.

Build him UP don't tear him down cuz it's only gonna hurt you in the end making him a clown

If Hillary'd gotten in all women would *feel* president and woulda made hell on earth for husbands.

Grace Jones is another woman who says nothing. Be a mystery not flashy but so embarrassing.

She's older, divorced, an actress and a feminist--Poor Harry, she'll control him, that's how this is.

The new trend: men going for older moms, that's what they want in relationships now: wow.

Bullying create hermits and emotional damage. The worst bullies are women = lifelong baggage.

LE FEMME and the Communist Spirit

Learn to cook then get any man because they're so sick of feminists who couldn't care less.

No events, I just wanna enjoy all my moments in the home thank you

You want me to go where, when it's so inferior/boring compared to my own home? Oh come on...

They're all sick powerless people looking for other people to control.

Not raised by dad but mom who makes her hate him/all men she's suspicious of every little thing.

You can take down a country thru war and pestilence or thru rank and uninformed sentimentality.

Once committed to immorality it's nearly impossible to change course.

I don't hate Hillary I just wanna see justice done and I despise her doings, is that so offensive?

He calls his wife "Mama" and she treats him like a baby. Is this pathetic, what do you think?

For Life of the Mother abortion is justified 2% of the time but used as an excuse 98% of the time.

These liberals/globalists are so sick they call baby killing (abortion) and child rape "freedom".

Taught to be social and loving a fake personna took over and masochism-- letting people in.

LE FEMME and the Communist Spirit

A nation without dads raised by feminist twits should love their strong leader but it's the opposite.

People hated my husband for the same reason: disciplinarian, military man, gets the job done.

A nation of twits and cucks hate the true man since feminists and liberals call it an anachronism.

The true man is blessed by God to lead his family. If the woman fights that, wow what treachery.

When enontiodromia (system inversion) occurs you can't believe you were intimidated by her.

When momma ain't happy no one is but why does it have to be constant just cuz she's feminist?

Hate Trump? He's the strong man daddy you never had, raised by mom who made you resent that.

He's the strong dad, something we never had. Wimpy men allowed their strength to be denigrated.

They hate Trump cuz mommy made em hate daddy then feminists said men are evil and shady.

Look at the insanity of female leaders, letting floods of people in to wreak havoc on their peoples.

Liberal feminized men hangout with females not out of interest/love but it's all they'd have.

It's not so much women vote thru emotion but phony virtue signaling for temporary thrill of ego.

LE FEMME and the Communist Spirit

They wanna put the whole blame on men who are mild and rational compared to women.

They're sluts and proud of it, primed in the schools saying if you don't you're repressed/not legit.

The feminist thing is harsh in women as they fight with each other in a minute (female pugilism).

They hold each other down like crabs in a bucket. Genius blocked by female community of suckups.

Feminist gig is wildly weak without knowing it. Witches, bitches, raving maniacs out to get president.

Liberal feminized men hangout with females not out of interest or love but it's all they got.

A disloyal generation contradicts you. She expects to love your enemies and have you too.

Saw a picture of a dead child on the beach so millions were let in to kill, destroy and rape.

She's the kind who forgives by running to your enemies and spilling the beans to please.

See that sweet little old lady there, she's really a scorpion. See past images, that's maturation.

Little old lady bakes cookies/seems so sweet but can cause so much trouble you're up a creek.

LE FEMME and the Communist Spirit

Of course the scorpion's gonna act like a kitten that's the whole thing while they're manipulatin'

A family of mostly women chooses one victim and when he dies another is chosen: scapegoatism.

Don't think a little old lady is harmless and can't cause trouble: they've lived/smart, double.

If you criticize her behavior it means you don't like her: refusing correction marks the immature.

Men aren't catcalling ugly women with purple armpit hair who swear so stop you false accusers.

All feminists have an anecdote about the horrible cruelty of men but men are nice, it's THEM.

All men are sinners that includes sweet little old ladies too: we all gotta repent, that's the truth.

Art is to uplift, show us what God is, thru beauty feel bliss--not this s--t by liberal twits.

Going around acting tough, who are you kidding it's just media fluff and we've had enough.

As an enabler she "can forgive anything" then puts you down because you draw the line.

Justin Trudeau's a globalist puppet taking mother and father outa all docs and you like this idiot?

LE FEMME and the Communist Spirit

Globalists have mobilized feminists to destroy the family unit and the father is **KEY**: the head.

Incompetent, dullard or mean mean are role models. It's in all the ads and confirmed in schools.

The feminists have been burned by men/hate all men and our answer is to embrace **REAL** men.

Men victimized in divorce court and no-consent abortions: Father's rights are nil, an abomination.

Dad your role is most important and don't let man-hating feminists tell you otherwise/evil disguised.

Liberals love to diminish the role of fathers and compare it to the saintly mother but dad is head!

They put down fatherhood because it is masculinity, their only defense against enemies.

Illuminating: The lady on the left wants to make everything look nice and refuses to criticize.

Women can't replace men and dad was the gentle loving one while mom was a raving harridan.

Women are inferior thinkers without logic or presence but those who break thru become the best.

Women have poor character cuz it takes strength to restrain from greed and that's the arbiter.

LE FEMME and the Communist Spirit

She couldn't resist what she did cuz she is what she is—the wicked never question their wants, sis.

A Man is created in the image of God: righteous, unafraid of adversity, protective of family.

Masculinity is destroyed but also femininity: sweet little ladies not tattooed freaks so shady.

Both genders are being destroyed, eaten up in a big blob empty vortex of crude blandness.

My so-called friend (feminist) would always befriend my enemies. We gotta choose sides, see?

They think they can have things both ways--it's doublethink saying it's ok to be contradictory.

They can't help it, if acting that way it's demons and unthinking reflexive actions/good riddance.

It's always about what's good for them not what's right.

You're not yourself, you're MOM for we become who we're angry at. Forgive/be released/be glad.

How low the left goes: Ivanka can't be a feminist wearing heals and a pink dress let alone a bow.

Women belong in the home and you can't get me out of it while few get in: home maintenance.

LE FEMME and the Communist Spirit

Man is to be over the women but in most homes he's under her domination = demons.

Liberals are big in making up stuff and calling it spiritual when it's occult and the end is miserable.

Feminism warps the minds of females and blocks interest with males and thus birth rate fails.

Feminists are against beauty pageants as dehumanizing but not pornography? Fascinating.

Those behind feminism/pornography are the same--both wannna destroy the west by what they say.

Feminists want to pull down beauty and pornographers treat beautiful women like whores, see.

Stupid liberal female politicians over Germany, UK, Scotland and Wales: an experiment to fail.

I know by looking at her. Can you really know a book from it's cover? Yes it's easy/can't love her.

They are indistinguishable from each other and claim something they are not, birds of a feather.

It is so necessary for female psyche to feel virtuous and loving they willingly let in the enemy.

Pathological altruism/empty virtue signaling combined with social equals women, what a shame.

LE FEMME and the Communist Spirit

Leader females: could they be dishonest, communist, globalist, socialist open border shills?

Image degraded by so many words of lengthy explanations from inflated self-importance.

Female politicians have no morals and seek to eradicate cultural values, they are of no use.

Esprit de corps: need family cuz a nation without fathers raised by liberal mothers made us empty.

Signaling virtue but into pornography and acting out too—contradictions of modern females.

Since body is endlessly mutable why not control it totally though feminists call it unacceptable?

Why no morals? Cuz they're liberals who think they're good and true morality misunderstood.

True morality is what God said not what you want, desire or prefer to believe.

I'd gladly give up mine to block female vote cuz what they foolishly choose is a fact/STAT.

Fools/female politicians love to hear applause when signaling their virtue and it's self-reinforcing.

That female ego beams with the audience applause and it's so sickening a contradiction.

LE FEMME and the Communist Spirit

They were raised by their liberal democrat mammas so they reflect her not the dad for balance.

Men tend to follow principals in politics, women not: it's all about emotion as the nation rots.

If the husband loves God even more than her she will never leave him/only him she'll adore.

Men know women go wrong but are too weak to confront them—you're supposed to be the head, man.

Wimpy men could never truly be a friend to women it's just mutual feelings of persecution.

I appreciate how you wanna share the burden by telling me all that stuff but please shut up.

Think of all the women needing self-forgiveness for abortion--hating self, life, being an ex-mom.

Diet restrictions are unnecessary hell. Eat what you want then don't eat to tomorrow = swell.

Obesity is not female empowerment just sickening.

If a woman can cook she has it made. It makes a home and they'll love her truly, no charades.

Gender dysphorics are deranged symptoms of a general social decline who do deserve this.

Any man who says he's a liberal is a woman. Jesse Lee Peterson

LE FEMME and the Communist Spirit

It gives em a thrill to virtue signal and be good. They don't care about the high cost, understood?

Feminists have been in control for so long they can't accept a real man in there so they hate him.

Feminism represents evil for last fifty years so it should be interesting now a real man is here.

Feminists have been all for killing babies and women having sex with the neighbor lady--shady!

God works thru man to woman so evil wants men to be women, the worst thing for everyone.

Mothers destroy sons (under guise of helping em) by hating the father or anger from ancestors.

Feminism destroyed families by degrading the conduit of God: thru Dad came God's reality.

Her mom turned her away from her father so now she hates all men and makes her son hate him.

Fatherless boys become Satan's toys cuz they lost their rudder and can't win in encounters.

Everything is in reverse. Weak men following wives around like boys or puppies or worse.

Two celebrity hangings in one week both connected to Hillary Clinton--what are we to think?

LE FEMME and the Communist Spirit

Fatherless females hate men, masculinity, discipline. Logic gone too since that comes from dad.

Fatherless females are like a rudderless ship and tend to promiscuity for a feeling of kinship.

Dad teaches restraint (don't hit girls) and brings focus, logic, reason, future vision to our world.

Dad just wants to be: tranquility in a happy home with thee. But feminism is divisive, you see?

A Man is different from a girlie girl, soyboy, beta male, gigolo or a liberal.

How are you a Man when you voted for everything a godless liberal female would like abortion?

In the fifties women were sweet little ladies and all were happy but now they're harridans/raving.

Natalism: Culture centered on the children but feminist anti-natalists die in the historical dustbin.

Equal outcomes is the highest virtue of a feminized society but brings such devastation, oh my.

Feminism disincentivizes men.

Woman from fatherless home will hate masculine authority and mimic her harridan mommy.

LE FEMME and the Communist Spirit

Mom is **ANGRY** and makes you hate dad, all men and life since she ruined homelife thru strife.

Why is mom so angry? Because she's alone, has to do it all, no **REAL** home/no one really cares.

What is an insane asylum: a home with kids (and pets) raised by liberal feminist moms.

Had a wonderful marriage, family/home and brought it down encouraged by feminism all around.

Feminist moms encourage terrible things like homos, masturbation even abortion: abominations!

Feminist moms are terrible teachers of debauchery and disgusting past times like Harry Potter.

Crazy neurotic female brings down her own house. She's even happy being alone/dating a louse.

It's exciting and wonderful to create a home. It's the most superior job and has great rewards.

To think judges give mom custody when dad could inject some sensible reality/we'd be happy.

Even grandmothers use "F" talk, anxious to be accepted by younger folk. Disgusting, grow up.

Dad can't see the kids, she wants full control. That's the way all liberals are when reason's gone.

LE FEMME and the Communist Spirit

Men are nationalists (reason), women are globalists (controlled, bought, emotions are the gist).

Trudeau put mostly females on his cabinet to be "fair" with "equal outcome"-- Canada's done.

God over man, man over woman, woman over children: Good men brings discipline/happy home.

Bad men are not the head of their wives nor bring love and order into the family: unhappiness.

Feminist moms are **WRONG** on every single thing yet allowed to raise children to be insane.

Feminists hate all men, masculinity, logic, reason and approaching all problems the same.

Women are lawless: they want each situation approached by their many justifications/excuses.

Female geniuses are totally obstructed in female culture and end up with men as their nurturers.

Fake liberal tears over border babies when they could care less about separated prison families.

Rachel Maddow fake tears over border kids--never mind about daily murders in abortion mills.

Liberals don't care about babies they want power and wealth and to make us bend by any means.

LE FEMME and the Communist Spirit

Maintain your home reality at all costs. All help must melt in and not interrupt one bit, Boss.

She has too big of an ego to see how glad you are to be rid of her so just enjoy your reward dear.

Men rule by laws but women by excuses, justifications and a million words that are so boring.

Women were denied the vote due to emotional decisions not what's right and we see their spite.

The logorrhea of the self-justifier is an endless barrage and you must not give in: manage it.

Fatherless females are emotionally insecure so create laws that are so wrong for our culture.

The evil spirit in the house makes you think you want it but don't invert reality: just FACE it!

Angry women can't love: children of the lie.

Demon in the house: we mal-adapt by needing it more but enjoying it less until we see her DIS.

Women like Clinton who believe in abortion to the 9th month quoting the bible: despicable.

They're not thinking for themselves and that's why this is happening.

Now that she/he's gone I see it was a demon causing our aneurisms which are disappearing.

LE FEMME and the Communist Spirit

Feminists are cowards, they can't take the heat. Pin them down and they'll deny they cheat.

Tell em what they did wrong then a million excuses/they can't be pinned down. Slippery, I'm done.

Her endless bitching caused his aneurism cuz men ARE sensitive to their environment, ma'am.

Dad draws lines: don't hit girls, don't steal, don't even touch what isn't yours and life will be swell.

I was an angry woman but then realized I was lied to and got over it.

Jesse was an angry black but then realized he'd been lied to, and got over it.

Evil is angry and blaming other people. It's either evil or good: black hood.

You've been brainwashed to be angry, and lesbians and transgenders aren't real women.

Angry women have been lied to/bought the lie totally. Tho' a wrong premise there goes the energy.

She's focused on revenge and what a tragedy it's a woman's infinite dark wrath, and all that.

Maxine Waters is inciting mob violence and it's extremely serious, dangerous, treasonous.

Maniacal Maxine Waters, Mob Instigator

LE FEMME and the Communist Spirit

Is that a strong women yelling like a hyena? Making demands and trying to fool ya?

Flaring up at criticism is very female and men do it now, raised by moms who hate males.

Neurotic females resent their mothers then become them but forgiveness opens em up again.

Legalistic liberal female very angry not a strong person but watch out baby.

She's always playing victim like she has it bad and you're the cad, just say good riddance man.

Her kids after being around her weak character act disrespectfully, even violent mal-adaptors.

Raised by mom who hates men now. Resents her but becomes her 'til forgiveness bestowed.

What you permit you promote, what you allow you encourage, what you condone you own. Michelle Malkin

We become what we hate, so tho' he's sick of the bitchin' he thinks like Mama and becomes gay.

NOT ALL but most women under fifty are out of control and very immoral. Jesse Lee Peterson

Girlie men: To defy a demanding feminist woman is to say "no" to mama, so they give in.

LE FEMME and the Communist Spirit

You being a "male feminist" is a dead giveaway of your treachery to truth/it's liberal chicanery.

Jezebel can't help acting like a total jerk it's a matter of the spirit inside her.

I see what you're up against. A wild, foolish, gullible, group-driven little witch who's also a snitch.

Jezebel can't help being divisive, snide, backbiting, attention-demanding or manipulating.

Pussy hat women's marches are all for open borders, crazy witches.

She's not a backstabber it's the spirit within her but you still gotta cut her lose or bye bye future.

Female heretics--crazy women--confirm bad men calling it "forgiving" but it's w/out repentance.

Just because she's a little ol' lady doesn't mean she's not a heretic who can lead you up a creek.

There's such a thing as a Jezebel spirit and it comes thru male or female and is very treacherous.

The foolish female fawned over the wrong group-determined narrative and ended your marriage.

Anger went away when I forgave mommy cuz we always become who we resent/ain't it funny.

LE FEMME and the Communist Spirit

Woman belongs in her home. I could never go out there again, chemical pea soup of Babylon.

Jealous people try to get her away from home since that's her protection--refuse that direction.

They want me on their turf to compete. Not happy as a bee in my own walled territory in full glory.

Women don't know what they're missing not staying home, It's the only part of world we control.

Real men aren't liberals, only beta males are like those.

Mean-spirited Jezebel will add fuel to the fire. Once she knows your weakness she's a liar.

If Jezebel hears you're a jealous woman she'll stir things up to really incur that emotion/rub it in.

Everything is just the way I want it in my home, like climate control, warm not cold.

Due to feminism women have become pugnacious and it's reflected in mean spirited politics.

Jezebel is an insidious divider. She insinuates, mutters and points to make sure you hear her.

She witched so much against Trump now we all hate her. As usual they overreach with bad behavior.

LE FEMME and the Communist Spirit

Maxine never gets anything done but run her extremely wide bass-fish mouth. Donald Trump

The Jezebel Scare: She won't let anything stop her, is manipulative and interferes everywhere.

The Maxine Waters democrat fringe will effectively turn dems into republicans. Donald Trump

Jezebel: Suddenly she wrenches away all of your Self Will—not thinking anything of it, too.

You hired her, not the other way around. So who is she to block your will or be so fowl?

A Jezebel spirit makes you think you need her and it's very depressing but good to fear her.

Bifurcation: Everything splits into male or female. Even with homos one is always passive you know.

Men and women: natural partners or natural enemies? Mutually dependent all minutes of day.

Hurts to see spouse isn't with God.

The raging spirit of Jezebel is happening now with the manipulations of global control.

A backstabbing loudmouth liar (no matter their color) is a dog but I'd prefer not to insult dogs.

LE FEMME and the Communist Spirit

   Jezebel spirit divides marriages, families, churches and nations--a splinter factor/abomination.

Greedy overreach marks the leech.

Only remedy for Jezebel spirit destroying your life, home and nation: Don't get involved, avoid em.

Men are told the pathway to virtue is weakness and harmlessness, a most dangerous myth.

Liberalism is actually the spirits of antichrist and Jezebel, spirits of division and discord.

The new maid is humble and causes no trouble, the other one ran rampant telling all to the rabble.

If weak in sin demons flow in and like the Jezebel spirit you'll be compelled to meddle, divide, gossip.

Jezebel is playing you like a fiddle. She knows your triggers and Achilles heel so good riddance.

Question: Did God make man for the man, or did God make woman for the man? What is God sayin?

She knew your weak points cuz you told her, she couldn't resist getting you outa joint so drop her.

Good heavens what's gonna happen now that witch is running

LE FEMME and the Communist Spirit

 I wanna strong man not a girlie man or a beta male or a mama's boy or especially a silly liberal.

Women let him think he's in control when he's not--women are cunning and kids are screwed up.

Women are cunning, knowing broaching a subject directs his mind in the direction she's intending.

Get him thinking her way, drop subtle hints into mix, goad him here/there then give him credits.

Yelling won't work. Keep sweet and be smart then it's a smooth ride not a rocky road/curse.

Women want equality so yell to get it then he becomes sheepish/bubbling with anger beneath it.

Wise women know it's all in the approach. If on the attack he holds back so drop hints with tact.

Controlling man thru sex is witchcraft. She's a deep cavern/bottomless pit with daggers: fact

Mind like a steel trap and articulate ability to tear him down with facts, that's the feminist axe.

She tears him down, he grovels to get her back. From his low position she looks good Mack.

Since it's based on false narrative/virtue signaling they rail at husbands who just wanna please em.

LE FEMME and the Communist Spirit

She's not tough and strong she's angry and resentful. See the difference or life becomes miserable.

Women more articulate with steel-trap minds so easily break him down in a fight, until the violence.

They're so hypnotized by feminists they rail at husbands without letup and you KNOW THIS.

Quibble over words and it muddles the waters. Pin em down, can't be done on what matters.

Unless wife becomes a sweet little lady it's gonna be shady or he'll fall into girlie man or soyboy.

It's not manly to talk so much, you were raised by your mother (women are loquacious brother).

Not since the sweet lil' ladies in the fifties were they worth a dime but are destructive all the time.

Spirit: It all comes down to Jezebel IN her and it means horror, alienation, guilt and fear.

Her spirit: It all comes down to Jezebel IN her and it means horror, alienation, guilt and fear.

The Jezebel spirit is always implicitly man-hating. Are you kidding? She hates your good men.

Jezebel puts down your husband or insinuates you're under his control as the dominant one: Hah!

LE FEMME and the Communist Spirit

Don't waste energy in social spread but focus all of it inside--a home of nooks/crannies so fine.

Much of what we see now is not Christianity but communism with virtue signaling.

Women were home-centered but now it's all about going out and home-life has suffered a lot.

She always wants to go out/can't stand staying home so the dishes pile up and it's hardly like Rome.

Being angry and resentful she can't take it out on him (he's gone) so the axe falls on the children.

When she gets upper hand she wrenches all self-will from you and thus good marriages are few.

If you want a wife look for one who is traditional and strong enough to submit to a man to cuddle.

Liberal acts like a petulant child cuz father was absent, mother was angry and God defiled.

Love him like a little boy and he'll become a man because he can finally trust/love someone.

Matriarchal societies in times of cultural decay when the men are cuckholded and say "whatever, ok".

Matriarchal societies during cultural decay when the men are cuckholded and say "whatever, ok".

As women become macho and men girlie men relationships don't work cuz women don't like em.

LE FEMME and the Communist Spirit

As boys, couldn't deal with mama then marries fem and hell breaks loose repeating early trauma.

Liberal feminists hate men, more as they regress into cuckholded beta males and it's sad.

When you break down the family you open the door to evil. It's happened to black now white people.

You can talk against men forever but not one word about the female's role in violence or whatever.

It was a Greek tragedy between sisters and things got so bad as the FEAR drove em all mad.

Liberal women hate men, turn children against fathers & don't love what's right or brings honors.

A woman can lie and a man goes to jail.

Pass laws protecting women from men but none protecting men from women acting like vermin.

Every law they pass is against family and men yet we're not allowed to talk about this hellish den.

Women who love men--fathers/sons--see the truth about persecution of males/women have won.

Women won't admit to being a psycho B from hell but many act this out--does this ring a bell?

Women blame men for the worst stereotype of that gender--being violent against her or whatever.

LE FEMME and the Communist Spirit

Women are now inviolate, you can't bring any of this up--only the most courageous talk about it.

Women think it's cute to get back at men for "centuries of abuse" like it's victory for all of em too.

Female ego won't allow em to admit to this or to fess up and overcome it so it gets worse, see it?

Since mom was a raving lunatic I just figured it was comic and emulated it until I woke up.

Women have been given permission to be a Psycho B so proudly/blatantly act it out guilt-free.

What stopped me from being a psycho B was marrying a military man and then I was free.

Wow--women are slapping men in public and they even think it's cute to be so violent. Wake up!

When women slap men they don't expect to be slapped back and if he does he goes to jail: fact.

The more she gets from him the more she wants it: love, reassurance but then the violence.

She starts the fights if he isn't paying enough attention to her at night or any perceived slight.

It's a female demon that makes her out of control and in this era it's confirmed/rewarded you know.

LE FEMME and the Communist Spirit

Signs of a sick relationship: When you're with him, no pain. When not, feelings of torture again.

After getting all her love needs met, when he's gone that's when the real craziness starts I'll bet.

Fears of abandonment take over and she acts needy towards him, a huge turn off bringing rejection.

Without him she's alone with her thoughts--an endless tirade of insults seen as all his fault.

When alone she hates herself so then condemns him for it since that's the current narrative.

Women have been blowing up for decades and tho' it's no-fault to them the men will walk away.

Her thoughts are from her past which she thinks has all to do with him so he's endlessly sassed.

Women can overcome being a raving lunatic psycho B but first they have to wake up and see it.

Female demons even turn on their friends and if you've ever experienced this you know it man.

When they inevitably split up she thinks it's all his fault and won't accept any of it--what a nut.

After the split he tells of her lunacy and she says "it's all onesided--has nothing to do with me."

LE FEMME and the Communist Spirit

The woman's place is being the man's helpmeet but now it's all about meeting her own needs.

She never notices her contribution to the situation or crazy way she acted always blaming him.

If she doesn't accept her place and keep sweet she reverts to the other extreme in a dead heat.

A woman can grow up today simply by seeing the part she played.

Pray to God for forgiveness for acting like mother who you resented so you acted just like her.

Forgive by seeing what's driving them--for it's not them but this thing making a home in them.

To forgive her see the early trauma in her life making her a monster full of strife, and what a relief.

Domestic violence is most always pinned on men but never the woman who triggers it, amen?

Now is the time to turn the children back to their fathers if you can get past the abusive mothers.

Satan is doing all he can to put out the light of fathers as world goes to hell/only God can solve it.

We're taught in media/schools how males are evil/violent and men are so weak they go along with it.

I've noticed how women start the violence and men respond to it. Women should fess up you twits.

LE FEMME and the Communist Spirit

Having been taught it's all men's fault she sleuths to find more reasons to hate his guts.

Bitchiness/argumentativeness is a form of domestic violence.

Bitchiness starts the violence so keep sweet for happiness.

When men verbally abuse it's domestic violence but when women rail like a maniac, not a chance.

When a man finally meets a sweet woman he can't believe what he's missed after that vermin.

Women act as though he walloped her for nothing and it's confirmed by all movies and sitcoms.

Just the way you're talking in your comments proves the point of the female's verbal violence.

Caution: Mama's ornery today and everyone knows no one's happy when she gets that way.

Shoving, pushing, needling, falsely accusing and articulately tearing him down without mercy.

Women hate it when we generalize, they want a tedious case-by-case and never apologize.

Real women are not threatened by this info: they've either repented or see it all around ya know.

You cannot say what women do to men.

LE FEMME and the Communist Spirit

 He can be yelling and if she smacks him she gets away with it but if he smacks her it's prison.

With booze it's an atom bomb in the house especially when her fem friends see him as a louse

70% of divorces are wife initiated but how much was because her fem friends encouraged it?

Rarely do violent females go to jail but the male is automatically assumed guilty without fail.

Women jealous of men's "power position" seek to make things happen to ruin that tradition.

Godless/liberal/feminist women hate men so be honest about this so we can turn it all around.

Brainwashed with lies, men agree or are quiet about it and generations are suffering from it.

Though evil exists in both sexes it's not true what they've said about men so forgive you ex's.

For the most part women start the violence and men respond. Jesse Lee Peterson

Men represent Christ on earth for woman so must learn never to let HER push him to be a lemon.

Can't be logical with her always bringing up the dead past until what the hell you smack her.

LE FEMME and the Communist Spirit

Satan put women in positions of power while also restricting criticism and making men cower.

Myth: men are mean to women. Solution: pass laws so she can even lie and he goes to prison.

Things get so heated and he's no match with words so what's left to do but smack the girl.

Keep sweet, shut up, overlook, let things pass and love him like a child who needs you, lass.

Feminism originated to destroy the family not help women. They were happy in the home, nappin.

Good women are against male-bashing just as much as men for families are destroyed therein.

Women need men, men need families and children need fathers and mothers.

Criticizing women will have the FBI at your door. It happens and with time it's happening more.

It started with the female vote. Men would never approve gay marriage or teaching tiny kids smut.

It's set up in such an emotional (female) way it makes you look bad if you don't think it's all-ok.

Husband said "I can't make her stop drinking or I'll go to jail" so let her kill herself/family go to hell.

LE FEMME and the Communist Spirit

Men represent Christ on earth for woman so she must learn to never push him to be a lemon.

Women have power over a man so why not use it to encourage him? What are his talents, ask him.

Laws: women are protected from men but not men protected from women and murder's happening.

How can coed sports be equal opportunity for the girl? And yet women push it in this crazy world.

In coed sports they soften the boys down to not compete so tough with girls, destroying them more.

Strong family = strong society, weak family = weak society--and globalists know that unfortunately.

Marrying a military career man cured my prickly orneriness real quick and I was glad he did.

Female anger from unresolved conflict or uncompleted mourning seeps out in incremental bitching.

What modern women don't understand: a good man and having children is most fulfilling/gone.

Silly feminists are pawns of globalists--due to the bad influence they've been successful at this.

When men are lost they tolerate crazy women more, hanging on but things get worse with her.

LE FEMME and the Communist Spirit

Turn hearts back to fathers. The beta males, soyboys or girlie men were raised by their mothers.

Men are always apologizing I've noticed and it's because they've adapted to an angry feminist.

After an angry mother/two sisters and belligerent female friends I know very well what this is.

Women are supposed to be keepers of the hearth: Keep bad out and educate morals in youth.

Blacks and women: If they can keep you angry they can control you.

Good women are against male-bashing just as much as men, for families are destroyed therein.

Racism does not exist, it's a made-up word. Sexism either, men really used to want you girls!

I dare you to show **ONE TWEET** proving Trump is a racist, these are lies of evil liberals/feminists.

Fathers not around, raised by angry mothers then the big lie is completed by the race hustlers.

Keeping blacks angry separates their soul from God so they'll become unproductive/more mad.

Feminism is a false religion and the results on the female personality are really devastatin'

LE FEMME and the Communist Spirit

Finding a good woman is harder than finding a ruby in a haystack (or something like that).

As women take over churches the whole set up has changed. It's just new age crap and deranged.

Going against her natural/decent inclinations to refuse sex to the uncommitted she gets mad.

A "MAN" loves what is right with his heart soul and might and leads the way, ready to fight.

The Man is to be the head of his wife but liberals will never agree with that despite the strife.

Two thirds of colleges are women only cuz society caters to them--liberals are holding back men.

Ask em if the man is to be the head of the wife--they all balk, change the subject, mock or deny it.

Women use law enforcement as sidekick strong arm, the enforcer of venom against husbands.

Women love Al-Anon for an audience of diatribe against husbands, a gossip mill, venom land.

False accusation charges: the Domestic Abuse Business and the Child Molestation Business.

The whole system and every sub-department is geared up and dug in against men: see it friends.

LE FEMME and the Communist Spirit

Lost in the confusion of false accusation innocent men are put away every day, every hour hon'

Men are Christ on earth yet condemned by vindictive women in cahoots with law enforcement.

Vindictive woman is cheered on by friends and since she's geared to be social it brings her grin.

Judicial system hates men as well. Screw-men business is huge/movies confirm he's guilty as hell.

Men: No fathers/raised by angry mothers then marry angry wives who take em to the cleaners.

Wife wins good image (victim) with legal on her side with kids too and he's sunk/can't say a thing.

Why do so many men go against men/take her side? Without knowing details/to be seen as nice.

A man is not a liberal and any man who says he's a liberal is a woman. Jesse Lee Peterson

The liberal man thinks like a woman and calls the decent conservative "racist"

Since women don't know anything but slogans they use "racist" as rudder to control conversations.

Liberal men are cuckholded and immoral, they think like women and could NEVER protect y'all.

They act like the only differences between male and female is physical. WOW, it's fantastic/infinite.

LE FEMME and the Communist Spirit

The difference between the two sexes is so infinite and that's why we say "vive la différence"!

The poison of hate, blame and victimhood has destroyed their willingness to be godly and good.

Even churches have become liberal social clubs because women took over and you know what.

We have the classiest first lady yet liberals drag her down to the gutter as something shady.

The FLOTUS is stately and regal not an emotional wasteland of falderal.

"Just too dam bad about you" said mom the shrew and then I mimicked her 'til neurosis was through.

How telling, men's clubs of America all love the man. Shriners, Masons--they all love Trump.

2nd wave feminism/Gloria Steinem killed men's clubs so they ended up in strip clubs, thanks a lot.

MEN NEED women-free zones. These witches just wanna end good fun and of course control.

If the most beautiful women are men why can't we do it too friends?

I'd hate an argument with Whoopi or the other dames. I've had enough cat fights with the lame.

Like most women without information/debating tools, Whoopi lost it/went ballistic like a fool.

LE FEMME and the Communist Spirit

WOMEN: it's just easier for them to go with the emotional talking points and the facts be damned.

Women with keen intellect who break thru the pugnacious feminist haze become best, I'm amazed.

Outside of the home it's all social adaptation but when inside it's fun, relaxation and creation.

Feminism ruined so many great marriages. Kids and pets lost their homes too/so unfortunate.

If someone's pedophiliac it doesn't mean they act on it but it's still too much for most spouses.

Judge Jeanine is breaking new ground with this, we've all been a sad victim of liberal feminists.

Liberals play so dirty and they'll hurt thee.

Immigration at it's core is to benefit those already in the country. Floods of unvetted groups, oh baby.

Dictator Obama: social transformation without representation.

The View was weaponized disinformation to keep women dumb.

Crazed liberal females are vulgar and disgusting: "Get outa my behind and my vagina" says Whoopi.

Deranged lunatic Whoopi Goldberg thinks she speaks for all women but she doesn't/she is vermin.

LE FEMME and the Communist Spirit

Be sure before asking God to make it happen, it may invite predation.

Women divorce the men and it's mostly based on false accusation--it's Big Business to get em.

How do race hustlers get power and wealth? By yelling "racist" that's how

Pope washes feet of a wishy washy globalist view of Islam.

Just pull the plug they'll self-deport

You're famous with low lives so you think this is it but it's a ceiling you've hit/can't go beyond it.

Works like a top: accused of racism, we pay up.

Herd works off mutual energy like a flock of birds assuming the flight pattern is correct, surely.

Labeled our customs, culture/traditions as bigoted, intolerant, repressive and discriminatory.

If left approves cuz you reinforce their weirdness they'll love you but you're going to hell miss.

Cashmere allergy: There's just too many fibers, the reason for comfort yet chemical misery.

I get sick right away with cashmere, too much opportunity for toxic chemicals holding onto her.

Don't wear used clothes. Previous detergents/where they've been/who they are...think of it dear.

LE FEMME and the Communist Spirit

Send them back or they'll keep coming

A free society requires high IQ populations, and there is not one low IQ pop on earth that is free.

They obscure the doctrine of judgement cuz they don't want their sins judged, they love em.

Justin Trudeau has never uttered a syllable that was not a gross platitude of stupidity. Gareth Rydal

Ever noticed how the most popular are twits?

They hate Trump cuz hating white people is the trend but especially a patriarch worth billions.

They get power over you thru intimidation, so if you have no fear (like Trump) how can they win?

One can never know when he will be done until that moment he's done. Thank you Albert Einstein

News never tells truth cuz they don't know it, don't want you to know it or been told not to say it.

Grandstanding: Making videos about a tragic event and making it all about you instead.

Grandstand: Using your personal tragedy to become famous and rich (spot light on the bitch).

If you don't like it don't come here that's how it works.

Political Islam is parallel societies and radical tendencies.

LE FEMME and the Communist Spirit

The Jezebel spirit puts down your husband like it's a feminist thing: It's in most women, fear it.

He calls his wife "Mama" and she treats him like a baby. Is this pathetic, what do you think?

After forgiveness everything falls into place. You don't elect or plan are just carried away.

I didn't say I believed her I just told you what she said but you gotta see this messenger's pathetic.

Traumatized lose boundaries then the problem floods in creating insanity. Lesson: stay calm always.

We lost our defenses when told "they're all good" and to be welcoming to the depraved dunces.

Guests: they burrow in then can't get rid of em. Like fish after 3 days they smell, just sayin'.

Thrift store gems: the point is I can't know who wore them before me.

It's not so much women vote thru emotion but phony virtue signaling for temporary thrill of ego.

They wanna put the whole blame on the men who are mild and rational compared to women.

If you criticize her behavior it means you don't like her: refusing correction marks the immature.

They think they can have things both ways--it's doublethink saying it's ok to be contradictory.

70

LE FEMME and the Communist Spirit

You gotta make your marriage work for in these latter days the default setting is becoming jerks.

Many men marry a body and when it changes it's over but a spiritual connection endures all weather.

They have no respect for what marriage is all about.

She couldn't resist what she did cuz she is what she is—the wicked never question what they want to do, sis.

70% of blended families fail ending in divorce. Having been a (failed) stepmother I know this.

Men are weak cuz their dads were gone, brought up by mom--its her anger when they speak.

Would you wanna be married to you? Yet your spouse is required to suffer whether male or female.

You don't know what trouble is 'til you get into a blended family where there's no peace only dis.

A blended family won't work like a first-marriage one: identity struggles and jealousy triangles.

Culture is now anti-marriage even as they redefine it. Divorce is "in"--her fem friends encourage it.

With all these interlocking jealousy patterns one's health degrades and the nerves frazzled.

Tho' happy in simplicity a blended family is complex identity struggles, anger, balancing forces.

LE FEMME and the Communist Spirit

Satan's minions are often very good lookin' cuz Lucifer's handsome so always think opposite.

No matter what God can heal your marriage.

Women always hugging/screaming since they saw the housewives did it--please don't hug me.

Unquestioning, unconditional and pathetic maternalism of Merkel to foreigners/leech interlopers.

Without correct view their speech is so boring, hitting on the wrong points, showcasing.

In fact everything's that way, the incorrect view creates a mess and so goes also your enemy.

Studies show women are more violent than men but we don't hear much domestic violence against them.

Why is mom so angry? Because she's a feminist not a sweet little lady like those from the fifties.

Housekeeper make it shine/smell good not just push the dust around/not quite clean no-good.

Trudeau: male feminist caught in a grope. Watch the drama teacher get outa this one, the dope.

But the new maid does not-quite-clean, no sheen. House should smell nice and have a shine.

Part of the Jezebel Spirit is to disappear for awhile, to fear it, to wonder what you did to deserve it?

LE FEMME and the Communist Spirit

Holy Household. No more leaky boat syndrome (gossip, outgroup preferences) but home/gold.

Blacks are angry because they don't have a father in the home and reflect a bitter mother.

Since men don't like macho women, what's gonna happen?

I'd never ever leave you honey cuz I know you'd be lost without me.

That's the thing, you don't divorce husband cuz they suicide or become hopelessly lost, boss.

Most women below fifty are immoral and it's proven by what they vote for like abortion and more.

My Ph.D. in Streets: Small desert town filled with feminists, living in cabin way out to get away from em.

Just so she can be a social justice warrior for a day + 15 minutes fame she causes trouble, ok?

The biggest myths meaning death of a country: masculinity is toxic and down on patriarchy. START

Maybe that's her destiny, maybe it isn't, either way it is none of my business.

Grandstanding: turning the event into her stage or opportunity to virtue signal like a sage.

Alcoholism is where you're drinking more and earlier. "Post time" keeps moving up until it's breakfast with beer.

Self-forgive for all you did when used by demons sis (like when you henpecked husband/DISSED).

73

LE FEMME and the Communist Spirit

Frenemy

The more you shield yourself from reality the more you invite predation.

Lock the gate to be free of whatever's happening outside the gate--now *every* day is great.

You're a genius and it's obvious, they're dumb as rats but copious, we're falling into a vortex.

People did nothing but hold you back and trip you up so it's just God we gotta please, look UP!

It never shoulda happened ever but really, you didn't know any better.

Many grow up with rejection, no one wanted em.

To be a writer gotta go thru the ringer first: squashed and burned then of humans you've learned.

Everyone wants something and you gotta be shrewd to save yourself from a disaster happening.

Wild animals have become nocturnal to avoid humans and I've done that too to be a good student.

The wicked never question what they want to do, the righteous are restrained/humble too.

LE FEMME and the Communist Spirit

It hurts being a majority of one and it's lonely at the top but you must before you turn to dust.

Closer you get to just your own life--free of interruptions--the happier you'll be/no strife.

Since 1970 the American IQ has decreased four points from immigration, trauma and dying out.

Without self-knowledge of importance of personal boundaries my early life was one big trauma.

All you do is complain about people when all you have to do is lock the gate and block out evil.

Appeared at their cabin door with a shotgun: the proper stance when you can't trust anyone.

With sickness the household becomes ingrown and that is best because we're making gold.

Even the news isn't as interesting as your own mind so get offa that thing and muse, think, dream.

You're gonna make it cuz you're for the Highest.

You're not alone/forsaken but under God's wing, hidden.

Around the superior man everything comes into perfect order.

Other people judge, I size people up.

It is not Christian to accept their wrongdoing.

LE FEMME and the Communist Spirit

I'd rather you not talk than say nothing.

Facebook is censuring me so I'm done,but there's plenty to read here, hon'

They've been raised in postmodernism. They don't argue, they censure. Goodbye to my Facebook Era.

Herd works off mutual energy like a flock of birds assuming the flight pattern is correct, surely.

He may be cute but open his mouth and it's not astute but mediocre: redundancy in poser's suit.

Facebook/Youtube bans Infowars but keeps Antifa and Farrikan. Clear prejudice, unequal weights man.

Instead of repeating in your head "why" does he do things just see him as a budding criminal.

God gave me a fresh start--off the charts--and my past sins didn't leave a trace, He had em erased.

When I take the day off, creativity takes off--relaxation from work tension brings on creative action.

Have office hours and if you sit there and do nothing, *more power*.

Since internet is infinite I get hooked on tangents then mentally absorbed for weeks lovin' it.

Don't expect em to understand you, just be nice. If you're managing the herd it's not a fight.

"These people are insufferable" means kids/pets have to suffer em.

LE FEMME and the Communist Spirit

Satan and his children love to attack you personally since they lack God's true authority.

All who sin are slaves.

At first they really have it but then due to immorality lose it.

Creativity is a funny thing. It's brittle, oversensitive, can't be forced, vulnerable so get away I say.

I just must have total solitude--SOLO--to develop on my own accord as God designed/bestowed.

Altho' it should be the opposite, the traumatized melt down and let em in, increasing the illness/sin.

Traumatized lose boundaries then the problem floods in creating insanity. Lesson: stay calm always.

Porn addiction: need it more but enjoy it less. Thrills you one day but doesn't do it the next.

Even your own family hates your guts/reject you for being right. Good's called evil, overnight.

Grandstand: Using her personal tragedy to become famous and rich (spot light on the witch).

Though they'll deny/ban/block truth it starts to work on em and they lose power/creative juice.

As it starts to work on em (truth vs. dogma) they'll start to bloat and beautiful planes are lost.

What you have is years of experience and no one can argue with that so don't compare/never covet.

LE FEMME and the Communist Spirit

Just cuz the past was bad doesn't mean the future will be. Life is in stages while God is forming thee.

When they want you to adapt your work to their limitations--forget that, go solo and transcend em.

Once you know how fast things turn you are humble and unassuming and that starts your winning.

In an instant you can lose it all. Knowing that--living on the razor's edge--is what keeps you on top.

Don't wear the bruised past but open up to blissful future for if you carry it along you're dead sister.

Forgive past actors teaching you boundaries and solitude--they were spooks but it's what it took.

Forgive yourself, it was the influence of other people. You were just too weak and in came evil.

Forgive yourself it was a demon and you were too weak to control him.

What I've learned in life is people aren't nice.

You're gross in your approach and we'll never be in touch so good luck, rot.

It helps so much to know it was a demon cuz then there's no need for explainin' just forget him.

Hysteria is tied to *dependence*.

They're either family or not. We're down to basics and God said our enemies are in the house.

LE FEMME and the Communist Spirit

Sin destroys decades of your life and if He's given you up to it you'll have no control/filled with strife.

Treating children like permanent victims is a bad idea but the politically correct were taught that way.

To skillfully manage human relations you must first know about em and that's my reason for livin'.

It wasn't rejection they just reacted to your sin archetype then life filled in/they became busy overnight.

If you preachers don't mention sin let alone hell, how will they know/why would they repent y'all?

Those who think it's a predestined groove: work all day. Those who see it as free will: nothing to say.

I'm driven every moment by the (divine predestined) groove which gives me most fulfillment.

Have faith in your inspired work though it doesn't sell. It's just a test and only the future can tell.

The more important word: "No". The most important wisdom: People are not nice ya' know.

Joel Osteen is a "pagan religionist/quasi pantheist"--see, there are words for Christian vs. new agers.

A watered down gospel is no gospel at all. It's but a cheap sickening thing of no use to y'all.

More resistance = less motion in your life.

LE FEMME and the Communist Spirit

Repentance is the key unlocking your predestined groove. Stay in sin and there's no breakthrough.

Repent = fall into your groove. Stay in sin = remain a clerk, gopher, stooge.

Get the dogs and kids used to a routine so they don't expect you all the time, that's being kind.

All a man's ways are clean in his own eyes.

Bad parenting = poor social skills or likability = parent hates you more and everyone else concurs.

He got bad in memory's dark tunnel where he played it all out, a low archetype gross and wild.

Man is in a fallen state and it really gets ugly, but through Jesus it can all be corrected quickly.

They weren't hating on you but the demon within, yet it sure feels like that when in deep sin.

Lied to while in a fallen state: that's the device used to keep you in hate.

Don't try to be nice or elegant, just be decent and that covers it.

Do not EVER take advice saying to forgive everything without repentance for they are of Satan.

When you come to a new place put up fence/locked gate. No one can impose/it's just your place.

Psychic opening is Aperture Syndrome: locked in a higher dimension as past dissolves/it's fun.

LE FEMME and the Communist Spirit

You must now stand up for truth. Stop walking on eggs, bring light to your culture, thru you.

When men are emotional, have doubt/fear/anxiety about life/can't stand up it's all anger blocked up.

The most important thing for you to do is sit/dream and do nothing then wait for God's blessing!

They were able to guilt you like an ingrate cuz you went to their dam party, sealing your fate.

You were the one giving them an inroad. Your home became a leaky boat on the wrong road.

I finally saw it: Rather than having a happy Saturday in bliss I had to put up with your s—t.

Watch out for the spirit of familiarity where the maids subtly divide the couple employing them.

Keep distance. Don't be influenced just cuz he's cutting the hedge--there's reasons for this.

Broken homes, lost youth, substance abuse.

Attacks are amazing when you stand for truth. But despite their hazing speak boldly, do it.

The friend of my enemy is my enemy.

You sit on a pile of brilliant/creative work so now just wait to be discovered and repent you jerk.

LE FEMME and the Communist Spirit

How to maintain a home: Keep stuff out.

"I enjoy cleaning it because it's so beautiful and she keeps it so neat". KK housekeeper.

Keep house by keeping people out cuz in a minute demons bring down whole lot/paradise blocked.

The children of alcoholics have the devil in themselves, that's how Systems Theory works.

Nothing is too beautiful. Nothing is too expensive. Ettore Bugatti

Repent/self-forgive when Satan had the upper hand in your personality and your mind was a sieve.

When you saw it was wrong in that very minute you got over it and God does not remember it.

To God the past doesn't exist (He's in this moment) so just move forward, you were unaware.

Love your home, see it as your Throne. Choose who comes in but the very best is being alone.

It's contact = conquest. Don't let her back in or the template and distorted implant reconnects.

God doesn't love you as you are, He said to repent.

Never put household in jeopardy by letting in the less than trustworthy. Instead, have victory.

LE FEMME and the Communist Spirit

The minute you see your own evil and stop blaming people it's over and God forgets it, for real!

I was too weak/boundaryless. I let em all in and decades went by in a haze of meaninglessness.

I too lost my sanity from a spirit within me and it took years to see it/unravel back to first reality.

When I think of the pain she put me thru. Always budding in/coming over when I told her not to.

Real living is climate control or it's a s**thole.

My heart is very big and that's the problem. I take and overlook until I don't then watch out.

I take a vacation then come right back to it as a servant to God and I have so much fun with it.

If they demonize you cuz you don't agree with them that's a spirit, believe it.

Truth is lacking and he who departs from evil makes himself a prey but God knows there's no justice here today.

Forgive only with repentance then cover it, overlook it, never tell anyone about it.

Christianity is a middle eastern religion, yet how many are left?

Don't you wanna know what it was before advising me to forgive? Without repentance, are you kiddin

LE FEMME and the Communist Spirit

To me, a thinker, resolving contradiction is more important than eating, sleeping or just living.

If I don't resolve contradiction life is sluggish, I'm skittish, can't fixit till I resolve it and then I'm LIT.

No apology for evolving past your comfort zone cuz you're the dumbest person I've ever known.

I do what I do, and it's you judging me not me judging you.

The lady said "I'm never gonna answer the phone again and always wanna be locked in".

I've always wanted various rooms and views. I can no longer track too: just bible, music, verse.

After the big event (you were so jealous of) their lives were mowed down and their glory gone.

Relativism says we are all beautiful--stubby, short, deformed or fat but the truth says we are not.

Greek ideals: Not everyone's beautiful but we can all aspire and dream and that's wonderful.

We are made in the image of God--we can do anything! But sin degrades that: ugly, fat, stink.

After being shattered I finally figured: it'll all be ok if I stay away.

LE FEMME and the Communist Spirit

Oh, the difference no longer being eclipsed by others I let in when I was weak/let down my guard!

Is being noticed a form of success?

Self-restraint, superior routines and tricks for creativity-inducement all mark the intelligent.

If things aren't sailing then get away, stop, turn on the music, look out the window: now all is ok.

After being so messed up in original pain what took it away was a locked fence and now I'm all ok.

Calvinists don't wait for anybody. Start your bible study on time don't adapt to their laxity.

Success isn't fame/fortune it's *insulation*. What made me free was not money but a fence/protection.

Just look out the window and music is optional. Don't let your mind be tracked by details ya know.

It you've great talent, sex sins will diminish and end it--must conserve your energy to make it.

Talented but simpleminded are swept up into filthy culture producing a lackluster, pointless career.

You're cute now but give it a little while, you'll show the ugly sin effects: look at Johnny Depp.

LE FEMME and the Communist Spirit

How to work: party first. Leisure is key to genius creative action, it's been proven by the best.

Relax, all the crap you did was due to demons now gone so with this remorse, be done.

You're too explicit fighting sex sin. Have some class, bring beauty back, don't make things worse.

Weekends are right brain: the magic of Saturdays when mind is untracked and can roam unchained.

So as a creative artist I start my weekends on Tuesday or even Monday. Then it's all creativity.

Self-control is a fruit of the spirit and a strength. Without it you're pulled down with no success.

Stop being impatient, your getting better and better every moment so just relax, it's epic.

Don't adapt to them in what you say. Every moment define you're own way-- too compliant, not ok.

If a genius you'll find your greatest success in the right brain not the left, it's all a unique gift.

In a very short time watch them fall though they look great now.

Stop being a leaky boat giving your energy to this or that affection, get in gear, do somethin'

It's what you do. It will turn fun as soon as you focus so stop worrying about this/win the highest.

LE FEMME and the Communist Spirit

How people control you: by taking up your time and your mind.

Nothing wrong with living your own life though it may mean never answering/leaving/visiting.

The day you get your life back will be the happiest day of your life. No adaptation, no strife.

At first saying "no" brings guilt. But within a very short time you're absolutely thrilled/killed it.

Why graft them in, you were perfect before.

Let nothing track your mind, close every door. It's a psychic opening to eternity and to soar.

It's contact = conquest. That's right, the mere contact makes you the worst after being best.

Stay away, don't go where angels fear to tread. They know nothing but you're at your crest.

I like the crow in the mornings, the crickets at night, the cows walking by but to humans, byebye.

I just made it all available to ya'll and I'm patient but soon you'll see the rare value/it's a mint.

You don't judge on appearances but their works—what are they producing good or cursed?

It's not the end but the beginning of the end and you're at your apex (highest game) my friend.

LE FEMME and the Communist Spirit

 You don't hate anybody, you just wanna do your own thing. But to win the booty means rejecting.

Take control or they'll mow you under. Be strong cuz there's a severe undertow to human nature.

God judges arrogance let alone the evil chasm into which we've fallen--all planned/not by chance.

Stop your evil gestures. They're embarrassing, low class and gross--seek and act much higher.

Pot makes them normal, it holds them together. Then later early abuse comes back, a repeater.

Fallen Hero Syndrome. They admired him so when he fell wanted to kill him: inversions of humans.

Stop saying you're talking to the dead, that's necromancy and it's wrong, deadly, occult, nasty.

Go into solitude and they can't bug you anymore. Here's where they lose control so I recommend more.

Decades were lost due to a demon you got when you met him. Every day clean the slate amen.

Social nature is a mass of cobweb illusions of who said what to whom and I'm done (whew).

All my life no one would let me concentrate. They'd call my name, knock on door/call on horn.

Life is one big soap opera with people constantly finding out they can't trust someone, what fun.

LE FEMME and the Communist Spirit

Shut up: that's all I can say to past introjects, memories, botherers, interlopers, opinion leaders.

Talk/gossip all you want, witch. I'm with God now enjoying each moment outa your ditch and rich.

When you fall off pedestals it can be devastating. A sudden fall from grace in the human race.

It's not that I don't wanna be with you I just wanna be alone with no one around.

Relax into conflict, have a simple life, be as a child always in prayer and He'll do all the rest.

Let your work stand on it's own—not needing wordy sophistic explanations but well-known.

When conflict comes, relax in it. Don't get high, call or shirk but be still and see God at work.

Be still in the conflict, watch God work: be free, never having to worry about that one again.

Don't drink, endure the pain—instantly God takes over again. Remember this in the dreary rain.

Pray, He watches. Pray, He resolves/nourishes. Pray, you're carried in a stream as He encourages.

They can't help it. People in a fallen state do crazy things cuz Satan is their father: get this.

A gossip betrays a confidence but a trustworthy person keeps a secret. Proverbs 11: 13

89

LE FEMME and the Communist Spirit

 The intelligent see things as obvious that the other's don't--it's gonna be a problem so stay alone.

For good relations understand that others can't see what you see nor draw conclusions that quickly.

Problem with high IQ is other kids. Learning not to be arrogant you end up a nerd/unpreferred.

Don't confide in an angry person because when they gossip, they tellin' everyone/you're done.

In dense generations the intelligent aren't even nerds, just alien.

Your IQ is the size of the gun, wisdom says where to aim it and education is the ammunition.

Life success: Intelligence, wisdom and education. You need all three to effectively apply them.

You can be the greatest sinner there ever was but still hate it. Hate sin then soon be free of it.

Sorry I was offended by you not being religious--how ridiculous--but now I see you're the best.

Trauma doesn't lower IQ but makes em mis-use their intelligence molded by the wrong premise.

The more traumatized you are the less ability to use your natural intelligence (no knowledge).

It's called the "blessed hope"--we should be looking for the Lord all the time and yet we mope.

LE FEMME and the Communist Spirit

Getting a fence and a locked gate was the transformation as life went from bad luck to great fate.

If there's hope in you it separates you from the world as you purify yourself and wait for Christ.

I was like a fish swimming upstream, gulping and drowning. A leaky boat with evil spirits bugging me.

Many are social and love constant interruption but I was the opposite, it caused anger and frustration.

I wanted to go deep inside and that meant total solitude and even my pets knew I needed quiet.

Invasion of my privacy (coming over without calling) even hurt physically, inwardly angry.

I was too weak to assert boundaries from a unique need for solitude so progress could ensue.

The weakest thing I did was to let em in. I had every right not to but I really didn't see that then.

It's such a social generation that if you're inward (saint/genius) they'll hate you/smear.

I fell from a penthouse driving a jaguar to original system surrounded by haters filled with derision.

When sensitives don't assert boundaries (let em in) they invert to most social ending in tragedy.

Same addictive process to any poison: needing it more but enjoying it less while losing all vision.

LE FEMME and the Communist Spirit

People can be cruel until they begin to die then mostly humility no more invincibility or acting silly.

My office door reads "do not disturb" and "do not knock" but they do both so guess it's too much.

To work I have to be in the right brain and that means NO pressure cuz it's all mental hazard.

I'm jealous of my privacy, what's happening to me? said the queen bee always bugged by thee.

When I'm with em I have to adapt and it bogs me way down so thank you but I'd rather stay home.

We become what we resent. If we hate the mother we become just like her: e.g. angry, indecent.

They just don't want a woman to work cuz she's expected to be focused on the jerks (like a curse).

Whether or not it sells is no barometer so stop asking me that and get real cuz I still have zeal.

To finish all you must do is focus. Nothing to figure out, same simple skills done when highest.

Nothing to figure out--just focus. You've already done it just make it perfect then genius relaxes.

To get the most outa each moment I gotta be alone cuz it's so deep and involved as it spirals down.

LE FEMME and the Communist Spirit

A neighborhood of self-contained households--not necessary to go door to door telling all.

Supply all his needs, leave him alone. Give him a work space, pray then you are done.

How to work: Learn to release mental hazards like people dropping in--no more of that friend.

If your home is office and you don't have a sec to block em must learn boundaries on your own.

You had the devil in ya and it was horrible, blight on America but Jesus erased it all, remember?

What's wrong with it? It takes hold of ya, you're possessed by it, always thinking of it--the pits.

Two trees outside my window are the tallest/most beautiful I've ever seen, breeze thru leaves.

I bought the house to stay in it always and never have anyone around.

Stop braggin' about how you keep nice home or get things done because trouble may come.

Even asking me a question is a mental hazard from then on.

I do not live in a social reality that other thing was just an emergency.

Just the fact you went thru it means you had to learn it since knowing it you'd never succumb to it.

LE FEMME and the Communist Spirit

Don't panic over work nor force the fit, it'll do you good to focus part of the day *then* get lit.

A home should run like a Swiss clock not chaos. If people are dropping in that crap must stop.

By loving your home you stay longer on earth.

Two separate nervous systems/brains: active vs. receptive. Tunnel-vision focus vs. wide/diffuse.

The problem with creativity is you can't force it. You develop routines to shake it loose instead.

Focus: Sit at work space, no interruptions, there to do a job, pray--this is empowerment.

No you can't force creativity but you can be smart and provide the space and TIME to focus.

You could be mentally free like a child or entrenched in a human system, a cobweb of illusions, wild.

My family were Calvinists: stoic, tea-totaling, thin, restrained, frugal, devout, routined, happy.

The Lord calls us out of bondage. That's outa the world and it's ways into His kingdom = fantastic!

If one isn't solidly with Christ God they naturally fall into satanic groove which is strange/odd.

What have you to be ashamed of? You love God, they don't--it's sin and sensuality they're made of.

LE FEMME and the Communist Spirit

You took our kindness for weakness. We feel sorry for you cuz once we start you'll end up passed.

The Spirit of Liberty has risen and I'm telling you it's the season.

To create you need a click in your head and that won't come feeling pressured/forcing the fit.

Relax, true creativity (from God) flows thru when supposed to then you will be through.

The minute I lock that gate I'm in heaven, my own little inner paradise: no interruptions, no more lies.

Knowledge of evil is understanding manipulation and distortion.

Since he's leaving the earth (dying) it's opened me up to new thoughts or what to leave aside.

Parents kill kid's pets without knowledge or permission, just given the information--a lifelong burden

Failure to launch syndrome: Not just not thriving but with parents you're living.

No one can accuse me of being angry if they never see me.

I don't do all the things you're doing. I just move from room to room writing, thinking, viewing.

Work not to give up—it's too easy to get into that slump.

He promised protection and peace and all he needed in return was your silent obedient consent.

Look away, ignore. Don't debate (mean fate) just walk away/close the door.

LE FEMME and the Communist Spirit

The only reason you keep leaving home is cuz you haven't made it into paradise, never to roam.

No I don't wanna go to a city or a party, and no I don't need any food. Just wanna stay home/cruise.

Just want my own life, reality, viewpoint, things, and SPACE. Life's happy only with a locked GATE.

When you say things that are dark, dirty or mean it congers in my mind so please stop/don't remind.

Don't give in or world goes black. Must be strong enough and mean it: "I don't want you back".

Bad associations bring/keep you down. With the mere contact (conquest) smiles turn to frowns.

Cut it off, nip it in the bud. Cut it off, nip it in the bud. You won't be alone and shoot up to God.

They're like a ton weight holding down a big balloon. You would shoot to the stars: boom!

Worst hell ever: blind inclusion. Biggest joy ever: discernment and exclusion.

It's priceless as the facade dissolves.

I can't work till I have a click in my head so I'll party till then.

It's a vague archetype in their mind then they fill it in (connect the dots) with misinformation.

All this time you thought it's ALL-OK when it's not. You think you're cool but you're rot.

LE FEMME and the Communist Spirit

It's their constant invitations/requests that control your mind and time, so be inaccessible friend.

Become refined and leave this grossness behind. Hear the crickets, birds, distant bells/so fine.

If I wait for the click in the head it'll all get done but if I force it none so until then have fun.

I learned about life the hard way, a Ph.D. in the streets about how to manage crazy people.

Everything bad I left behind in California but here I'm good cuz I won't open my gate to ya.

Don't give in to this crap all around because they are so off base and their declension is profound.

Yak yak yak, so self-important aren't they.

Just keep em away for one more day I pray.

They love social cuz they lack inner life.

The constant invitations are only interruptions to yours and God's plan so don't give in/refuse em.

After the event you have emptiness. It's addiction: needing it more but enjoying it less.

People die differently. Dad gave up to watch all day TV, mom looked out the window to eternity.

It's all fine and good if you wanna talk like that but I can see right through it.

If we're right we know we're right and don't mind saying it. That's not arrogance it's by studying.

97

LE FEMME and the Communist Spirit

Those who believe in God and living it are your real family now, not always by blood.

Cut it all loose in order to just develop on your own accord--that's what you need more of.

All my life I pined for him and now he's gone--what a waste of time/heartthrob.

Don't wanna buncha words I have to read. Just two sentence quips, please.

Like a thread unraveling a sweater to the end, so too the creative act completes itself/what fun.

Don't worry once the creative clicks you'll finish twice as much or complete it all instead.

By waiting for the click in the head you'll get far more done in the end.

I'm waiting for that click in my head. In the meantime, I'll party on and not think of it.

What ever you must do, put farthest from your mind then with leisure suddenly it all realigns.

Art: why waste time describing it, I wanna look at it.

Don't compromise, life's too short for that.

How to succeed fastest: wait as long as you can before starting until you feel you'll burst.

Can you say this: "I don't like you and want you to leave now"?

Hold back from work until it becomes a tidal wave inside, ready to burst forth.

LE FEMME and the Communist Spirit

It always helps getting away so keep doing it: take off work for the day.

Solution: ignore em.

Engrained in Marxism is envy, so in social generations solitude is the only way to stay free.

Hanging on to the person who is wrong makes you less fit when the right one comes along.

We acclimate to lower people then don't see the evil and become to the good invisible.

Constant invitations: as soon as you go to one potluck they invite you again/can never satisfy em.

You have nothing to fear against atheists promoting evil. See the truth and you're a protected people.

The enemy is the prince of darkness working thru others.

I'm not wasting time but girding up strength/relaxing into receptivity for the next creative surge.

I'm not wasting time I'm readying for the head click to start again and then complete to the end.

Look out the window doing nothing, now you're producing something.

I am waiting for that click in my head. I must have that click before I start. Paul Newman

It's not a waste to take a break, even a real long one--wait to start then it's like a holy spirit streak.

LE FEMME and the Communist Spirit

Like crabs in a barrel they wanna keep you trapped, weak and frail so it's time to cut it loose: sail!

Don't dismay cuz in the land of the blind the one-eyed man is king--you're smart so do something.

Pearls before swine: don't waste too much of your time trying to wake em up, draw that line.

It's not that I can't track it's that I refuse to BE tracked cuz nothing's higher than my own map.

Time is the most valuable asset to a successful life so stop wasting it with time-fillers and strife.

Shaking/trembling from recognitions. You don't know why, you don't have to know why, trust em.

Why would your intuition make you shake and tremble like that? Hold on, you're seeing the cad.

Paul said never rely on appearances. Recall wolves in sheep's clothing--trust these verses.

Over and again you saw him as a sheep and over and again he became a wolf and a creep.

Don't read/browse too much cuz it's all about a hunch (inside) so it'd be better to just retrench.

Dear Lord: I don't like it when You leave. I'm only happy when You're here protecting me.

"There's not a spot where God is not" is false/oneist cuz the holy spirit can withdraw in a minute.

LE FEMME and the Communist Spirit

Resist the narrative that's all around. Hold on to real values learned when you were young.

When you become whole it's fun dealing with attacks from haters cuz you're always the winner.

You're not Christian if quoting scriptures yet supporting everything wrong like Obama the raper.

Our whole problem is fools and fanatics are sure of themselves yet wise are full of doubts.

Your work must stand on its own/not require your three page explanation but that's "art" in the nation.

The fact that they're all so wrong means you being all so right will float to the top overnight.

It's good vs. evil and good will prevail, people! Must know we'll win, so stand high as a steeple.

The wicked do what their father devil tells em to.

Porn started in childhood, with trauma they ran to it--filled gaps biochemically, never outgrew it.

Everything wilts, everything fades cuz God gave it to us temporarily so focus on Him, truly.

Instead of hating them for what they put you thru thank them for the strength it built in you.

Looking back is going back.

LE FEMME and the Communist Spirit

Courage inspires you, even this *very* jaded generation of today cuz a flicker can turn to a flame.

Reminding people that they're dumb and have no answers is a perilous business. Stefan Molyneux

How can certainty submerge itself into doubt, promiscuity, uncertainty and selfishness?

"Opportunity cost" is a great breakthrough in rational thinking. Pests block the best/you're procrastinating.

Necromancy (talking to dead) is the occult--it can be tempting but as life degrades watch out.

We can't talk to the dead (necromancy) but we can remember what they said/wisdom-get.

Ancestor religions are necromancy. Wish it were true, to talk to dear old dad would be so easy.

Death is sleep until rapture. If we went up to heaven, we'd have to come back down for sure.

Talking to a dead ancestor it is in fact a familiar spirit and you've fallen before you know it.

We can't talk to the dead, they're asleep until the rapture when Christians will meet Him in the air.

Be sure before asking God to make it happen, it may invite predation.

People are known by who they like and admire so if you still love em after finding out you're a liar.

LE FEMME and the Communist Spirit

Get ready to die. That means to appreciate this day maximally and transcend all ties.

Leave time to sit and think. Just puttering is the most productive time: rising above rinkydink.

Let puttering and thinking be your default setting. Action reversing with diffuse attending.

The joy of retirement is switching from active to receptive mode. Profitable leisure: diffuse attention.

If you can't take it anymore it's time to retire to the right brain which is timeless, perfect, color.

"We're family" when combined with lengthy self-exaltations shows your immaturity and I'm sorry.

Don't addict to social approval cuz it stops you up. What moves you is disapproval, way to the top.

You're famous with low lives so you think this is it but it's a ceiling you've hit/can't go beyond it.

What is most important? Land and a locked gate, no adaptation to anyone or it's bad fate.

These people are freaky so why can't you see it?

Get ready to die. Leave facebook cuz no one cares here. Return to your own situation, nurture it.

Prepare for death tho' it may be decades off. This keeps you from useless tangents/those who scoff.

LE FEMME and the Communist Spirit

Above all block all time wasters. Now you're in charge and with people you must manage him/her.

Once you get into the right brain (cornucopia) stay there by refusing to be tracked anymore!

Even these news videos are a waste of time. Too circuitous/repetitive, just read headlines.

It's just temporal reality--let's go to eternity shall we? That was Einstein's major interest, truly.

Let your mind go with free rein. Don't let anything track it again cuz life is a pie, recall that saying.

No tunnel-vision: Stay in the right brain and when right time comes you'll move into happy action.

It's Holy Spirit Ease. The key to work is to WAIT cuz it's your creative spirit, destiny/fate.

I'm not gonna start till I hear that click in my head. Paul Newman

Keep shaking loose previous concepts. Switch to music, take a walk, become simpler--it works.

Genius is characterized by the capacity for leisure, would-be genius has incapacity (he only works).

Retirement is like taking off a straightjacket and putting on some cozy pajamas: ah, at last.

Anyone who does not believe in miracles is not a realist. Audrey Hepburn

LE FEMME and the Communist Spirit

 Grandstanding: Making videos about a tragic event and making it all about you instead.

After forgiveness everything falls into perfect place. You don't elect or plan just carried away.

Can't have fear and faith and those without faith can't please God so give up fear and be strong.

If you don't like it don't come here that's how it works.

Don't drink with work buddies cuz if they're trying to impress boss they'll throw you under the buss.

The deep/sagacious prefer old movies, why is that? No sex, boobs or tech effects (a hex).

Wretched behavior is when God gives us up to our desires/sins (and the compulsions therein).

Sometimes I get weak and the past is my guide.

Eat, sleep, write.

You are made so batty/crazy keeping people away but I thought you said you wanted fame?

Guests: they burrow in then can't get rid of em. Like fish after 3 days they smell, just sayin'.

The more hands on deck doesn't make it more efficient, more often they're a burden darn it.

Why can't we trust anyone? Due to the total depravity of man until he's saved and begins again.

LE FEMME and the Communist Spirit

To skillfully manage human relations you first gotta know about em and that's my reason for livin'.

To be a writer gotta go thru the ringer first: squashed and burned then of humans you've learned.

I don't know why God chose me to be a vessel for a Creative Act but it's a real miracle in fact.

If you're a writer you write and if a painter you paint. Stop saying what you are if in reality you ain't.

Don't give em the time of day, the dumb. They know nothing and waste your energy. Walk away, gently.

You've got to stop work to "take distance". Get away from it, see it differently, RELAX.

You gotta choose sides. You can't have both worlds cuz God's wrath on you will fall on me.

They're either family or not. We're down to basics and God said our enemies are in the house.

Everyone wants something and you gotta be shrewd to save yourself from a disaster happening.

Is there anyone out there who understands, anyone? You all seem half asleep and unconcerned.

Put cat doors everywhere. They have their own underworld--enable and appreciate it, share.

Life is a wonderful opportunity to let God come thru thee in a Creative Act making them free to be.

LE FEMME and the Communist Spirit

Take a mental vacation for where to escape? Your home is a palace and outside it's dangerous.

Wild animals have become nocturnal to avoid humans and I've done that too to be a good student.

Ph.D. in Streets: Depths of hell seeing horrible things and people so now that you know, be sweet.

The most productive time possible is through productive puttering or just looking out the window.

If you have pets you gotta clean up after them. Establish routines then life is happy and fun.

I just wanna think without any interruptions whatsoever. Cats/dogs are bad enough, whatever.

Time to stop/look at the wind thru the trees and that'll shake everything loose so you can see.

Art is to edify not to disgust/make us wanna die.

It's not I, God has gifted me but not for free.

We are made in the image of God so all they do is degrade that image--don't degrade if yourself.

They're already reprobate if can't see God in the heavens. An orchid, a star and they're doubtin'.

Don't worry about it--be on vacation, always. That is the right brain like a child on Saturdays.

LE FEMME and the Communist Spirit

The reason people don't answer emails is they just don't want to/they've got too much to do.

Real men and real women are always right cuz they're guided by what is right and SEE what's right.

It's old fashioned to do what's right and not do what's wrong, it's whatever works in the throng.

All angry people are prideful and can't know God for pride is the nature of Satan. Jesse Lee Peterson

The wicked never question what they want to do, the righteous are restrained/humble too.

Angry people can't love cuz anger is the nature of Satan and his destruction.

I understand it but can't live with it. Admit to yourself you're playing God and wrong.

Forgiveness is the most important since it's disburdening you of a lifetime of distorted implants.

An entire lifetime you've been carrying this around. Forgiveness is success/new dawn.

Forgive only after repentance or create criminals.

Think of how long you've carried this burden then see the power and efficiency of forgiveness.

Forgive them (know not what they do) so God forgives you (released for success in all you do).

LE FEMME and the Communist Spirit

I forgive you totally but can't live with ya, Nutty.

The strong have internal strength (it's called restraint) while the weak man gives in to everything.

It hurts letting people go but recall why you did it: moral ineptitude like it's bred right into it.

Ego is blind. It can't see how transparent it is in a bind and it's embarrassing to those with a mind.

Kept forgiving her greedy overreach each time more, then of great danger I became aware.

Marriage manual by KK: End every sentence with "honey" and talk to him like a little baby boy.

Just sitting and thinking is working so don't let em ever say you're not accomplishing anything.

No mercy without justice. Forgiveness not a free pass to repeat, must turn from wrongs you idiot.

Parents: Whatever you are the kids become. You can't hide the fornication it's a spiritual thing.

Stringent order (they hate that) makes me so happy and puritanical order began our culture.

Leave the path open don't plan a thing. Zero, vacuity, open: that's the highest way of thinking.

Protect yourself cuz whenever they get the upper hand they'll take all your stuff.

LE FEMME and the Communist Spirit

Be still and know God. Your over-reaction to the problem is the whole problem so stay calm.

It's amazing how a tiny thing in the environment can wreck your life and reality in a minute.

Just think, you never have to go thru this again.

Overcome anger then see what's going on.

You've got to tell the truth because we're fighting against evil.

Like shit on the shoe or fish after three days they just won't go away: you must insist or die.

The righteous man is delivered from trouble, in his place the wicked man goes in as a ransom. Prov. 21

Oh the feeling of going beyond a person/problem! Like a cornucopic paradise of bliss opens.

Most important part of house: locked gate, wall/fence.

Path out of insanity is unique. You must unpeel distorted implants that put you up a creek.

The maid did it. She had a demon in her and we went insane adapting to it. Wake up to this.

Insanity comes from mal-adaptation to the larger system not something inside of us happening.

What is the mal-adaptation? Listening to them, taking it on, mimicking the debauched/sick throng.

LE FEMME and the Communist Spirit

What is the mal-adaptation to the school system who says anything goes? Becoming most low.

Evil is rampant roaming thru the earth seeing who to devour. Warning: be careful every day/hour.

People are psychos, really gotta watch em. Don't let em in they'll do you in. It's who they are/in sin.

It's the contagion of lunacy: in adapting to the crazy maid we actually need her approval, hey

You betrayed my trust. Once you got the upper hand you took my stuff.

Social? Our life is important too, in solitude.

Once the anger is gone (realizing it wasn't right) you come into the light, everything's outa sight.

After 33 years desert wilderness I learned solitude in nature then moved to my new paradise.

Look out the window and ideas come up. Be tracked by a movie in a groove and I'm blocked.

It's not that I don't wanna be with you I just wanna be alone.

Strong work ethic shoots outa bed and works all day. The lazy just wants to hangout and waste.

We adapt to problems by becoming blind to em and that's where the trouble starts so fire em.

They're either good or evil so tell the truth/don't be angry. They'll either wake up or run away.

LE FEMME and the Communist Spirit

Just think you'll be 40, 50, 60, 70, 80 then eternity with a brand new body.

Humans only examine their core delusions after an unbelievable amount of suffering. Stefan Molyneux

Wrong, fruitless or selfish decisions brought God's wrath—an ungentle goading, I remember that.

This is how it works, count on it. How do I know? I went thru it.

A seared conscience loses discernment between right/wrong, good/evil.

Biggest reason to forgive (and not just for lent): we become what we resent.

You are not only responsible for what you say but what you didn't say. Martin Luther

If you hate someone it could be petty competitive strivings that keep you from benefitting/loving em.

If you love em (kids and pets) they'll all get along together too.

It's demon possession they can't help what they do but nip it in the bud or you'll be dead too.

It wasn't you it was the devil but still you gotta get strong so he can't use you.

Stop feeling remorse/embarrassment over past cuz it was satan but now you're free/life's a gas.

Satan made you do absurd, ridiculous and evil things cuz your weakness made you his plaything.

LE FEMME and the Communist Spirit

It's demon possession, they can't help what they do but nip it in the bud or you'll be dead too.

The thing a little demon wants to do is gain your trust but not thru right action but wrongfulness.

For success disentrench from the system cuz it tracks your thoughts and you don't need em.

It wasn't you it was the devil but reinforced by this generation (debauched) it became a knot.

Just step into new life. It's crossing the Great Divide from the angry past to freedom from strife.

Step UP, rise above all problems. Fly above it like a bird looking down on these anachronisms.

Enjoy success, you deserve it. You worked, overcame, matured and walked away from it.

Never adapt to interruptions. You must now manage your time where they NEVER determine it.

Words connected thru meaning AND sound. That's the rhyme, it's higher than paragraphs long.

You shoulda watched what you said to me, and you thinking I was just like you! What an insult, fool.

They didn't hate you it was the devil in you so just repent and it mentally disappears from view.

If everyone hates you it's cuz you're a jerk so just repent then start your work.

LE FEMME and the Communist Spirit

No matter how good they look it's an illusion of Satan and it's ugly inside/take it in stride.

Listen Rustler just cuz you got away with it doesn't mean we're gonna forget it, believe this.

I'm real nice 'til I'm not so don't get me mad or watch out. American citizen

The children of God are your new family and the blood ties are no more, really. No tears, please.

Sometimes you'd like to see em again but how interesting: there's just nothing there to work on.

Satan makes you remember the bad. It helps to know it was a demon and never recalled by God.

Satan wants you filled with embarrassment, remorse, shame over a past faux pas/don't give in.

Love your neighbor as yourself, do what is front of you to do and then you will have a good life.

They become no more important than strangers on the street and after all your tears that's so neat.

Once they see you don't think like them they go out and tell everyone cuz that's just evil humans.

Once your cross the Great Divide blood ties mean nothing and the spiritual ties everything.

Everyone's into "family" and it's a laugh, really.

LE FEMME and the Communist Spirit

Out of many I had **ONE** family member with spiritual connection surrounding the Savior.

My **ONE** family member brought me to a whole new life while the others just kept me in strife.

When they're not children of God (born again) they're not family anymore/free of that.

In the twinkling of an eye you have nothing in common with her/him and that's how God does it.

When they're not children of God (born again) they're not family anymore and we're free of em.

Jesus came to divide us, don't forget that. Whoever tells you it's to unite us is a liberalized heretic.

You can't ever be at their mercy or they'll impose stuff on you and it's smelly so always stay free.

In the twinkling of an eye you have nothing in common with him/her--that's how God does it sir.

You don't move in with em/burn all your bridges or let them move in without dates of riddance.

People are sinners, utterly depraved. But through Jesus we have God so repent and be saved.

Children of alcoholics are adapting to the devil. Alcohol is a conduit to him and it's awful.

LE FEMME and the Communist Spirit

No one wants to see their own depravity but weakness allows demons to work it thru us, see.

Humble yourself, pray, seek His face, depart from your wicked ways: God heals you *and* your land.

Thank you God for exposing, tearing down and replanting.

It's the divide and conquer lying spirits that prevail in this age, it's called the Strong Delusion.

Lord expose the whole choir of evil doers and remove them for our future.

It's easy for the world to seduce your kids when they see you as hypocrites.

Our predestined groove can only be found thru repentance, or miss the boat and stay a nuisance.

God is really comin' thru you now you're getting ready to show/make the dough cuz you know.

That's right: One night of sin and your whole life changes overnight.

Being gone so long they see you as enemy.

Should feel secure in our territory. Reason your dog knows he's home for life: he trusts you, silly.

God put it in you: a SEED. Let it grow, design and nurture it--who knows where it's gonna lead?

RECAP. How to succeed greatly: humble yourself, pray, seek His face, turn from wicked ways.

LE FEMME and the Communist Spirit

Your talents should be as simple as a bird singing. It's holy spirit ease: naturally, effortlessly.

Not just your talents but your team is predestined. That gives me a good feeling, not free-willin'.

LEARN TO SAY: "She did this to get back at me" Always see everything as a device then stay free.

Good-looking and glib smiling preachers are successful because they're one with the devil.

Tho' we'll always be sinners, gotta repent of the major ones (holding you down) or you're a goner.

Forgive (overcome obstruction). Become your first nature again, the sweet child people were lovin'.

We're not to respect and include the sinner but withdraw, restrain, draw lines, be an overcomer.

Cat's aren't independent, hon'--they get mad if you're gone too long.

Forgive yourself for anger cuz you couldn't help the demon blowing up, an archetype growing up.

Puritans restrained unhealthy tangents like porn because they wanted to stay high with God.

If you love your child teach em to be likable to others too then all life is happy, loving and cool.

No other religion gives solution to man's fallen state of abomination but Christ and it's simple.

LE FEMME and the Communist Spirit

If you don't have place for something don't keep it but many homes are storage bins/trash pits.

Don't knock, don't come up the stairs, don't bother me. Protect my privacy not make me crazy.

No other religion gives solution to man's fallen state into abomination but Christ/it's simple man.

Common sense comes from God not man.

We're waking up and dumb is getting smart. An evident change: in brain-dead there's a spark!

You're my friend if you love America, Trump, freedom, God & If you hate these things you're out.

The unit is household not neighborhood. Don't spread out (social) but focus therein, that's good.

If you love God you're my sister and if you're my sister and don't love God you're not. Rot.

Jesus said don't even go to the funeral if they didn't love God like you do.

God is all that matters so if you don't love Him blood ties are irrelevant, meaningless, shattered.

Know thyself in this spiritual battle: Do you do good/refrain from evil?

God takes the spirit of anger from us when we realize the reason we were, and it's an oasis.

LE FEMME and the Communist Spirit

Don't feel bad about the times you went off the deep end for it's like a trance, you were lit/in a fit.

Forgive yourself it was just a spirit in you. When we get weak it comes in/destroys more than a few.

You answer a call in them like an echo and suddenly you're in fame kiddo.

Creative process: I know it's God when it starts and I know it's God when it stops thank goodness.

They change things all of a sudden like the monkey's on Chance's Island.

Monkeys learned from apes across the sea--sudden and telepathic. In humans: decent vs. barbaric.

Forgive yourself for when the devil was in ya. You got weak then he did his business thru ya.

Either I'm skiing, or it's chaos. Tanner Hall

I don't have to explain it I just resonate with it.

I hate computers cuz it reminds me of school. C.R. Johnson, Pro Skier throwing trix off mts for big bux.

There's nothing done that hasn't been done before. Don't take it seriously since you've repented dear.

Anything that tracks the mind is not satisfying. You wanna increase inner amplitude by opening.

LE FEMME and the Communist Spirit

It's culture or sexual licentiousness, can't have both. Culture (like reputation) can vanish like smoke.

Every insane thing I did was from society's input. Left to my own I woulda been ok from head to foot.

God said I don't remember you doing it and I didn't see it cuz I erased it through My Son I sent.

I suffered all my life from rejection for being conservative but didn't know that was why it was.

Weak in character just slide into the gutter if that's the narrative cuz they know no better.

Established writer is elegant all day but ultra comfortable cuz it's constant having something to say.

Don't even sprinkle it once in a while with F-talk. Never or they'll peg you and career will stall.

If they don't support your work they're in opposition/will undermine it so drop blockheads/twits.

He called my freeski movie corny and I said hey if they can do that they've a right to be.

Give em a little so it all seeps in then tomorrow teach em again.

You're not alone and forsaken but under God's wing, hidden.

Shake it loose: do everything differently than you've been doing and you will see.

LE FEMME and the Communist Spirit

Get ready to die. That means to appreciate this day maximally and transcend all ties.

Prepare for death tho' it may be decades off. This keeps you from useless tangents/those who scoff.

Oh well, just forget it all and look out the window. You've got a locked gate so they can't get to you.

If you're a writer you write and if a painter you paint. Stop saying what you are if in reality you ain't.

I don't know why God chose me to be a vessel for a Creative Act but it's a real miracle in fact.

Ph.D. in Streets: Depths of hell seeing horrible things and people so now that you know, be sweet.

Think of how long you've carried this burden then see the power and efficiency of forgiveness.

Don't embrace complexity thinking you serve the world. Make it simple to remove the curse.

Just one day without news or anything else online--now I'm rid of the blues and feeling so fine!

Always return to music as your default setting and soon you will branch to the right thing.

Just work then wait.

Impatience is the biggest problem, let God in, give Him time for the final day of victory/success.

LE FEMME and the Communist Spirit

A rising tide raises all boats but a sinking tide sinks em all too just look at Venezuela you fools.

I have felt like the underdog *helpless* as the foreign invasion goes on without cessation.

It's a mentality where virtue signaling reigns supreme cuz no one wants to be out of mainstream.

For success disentrench from the system cuz it tracks your thoughts and you don't need em.

It helps so much to know it was a demon cuz then there's no need for explainin' just forget him.

She's not a backstabber it's the spirit within her but you still gotta cut her lose or bye bye future.

You're in a new life and will never look back. Locked into a new dimension like white from black.

Your art isn't about politics it's about your generation's narrative of such--old slogans outa touch.

The left are sick freaks--we know that--but violently want open borders to totally wreck us.

We win on the war of ideas, they're so false they must rely on crybabies and bicycle locks.

700,000 homeless American kids and left won't lift a finger to help. Democrats, remove yourself.

Is that a strong women yelling like a hyena? Making demands and trying to fool ya?

LE FEMME and the Communist Spirit

Forgive (overcome obstruction). Become your first nature again, the sweet child people were lovin'.

I see what you're up against. A wild, foolish, gullible, group-driven little witch who's also a snitch.

Forgive yourself, it was the influence of other people. You were just too weak and in came evil.

The democrats love immigration due to false compassion and the desire to win elections.

Equal playing field tolerates buffoons.

The nasty EU stands for "tolerance, diversity and human rights" and we are rejecting them all.

Sweeter they are the more virtue signaling but God wants us bold/strong not such obvious faking.

Step UP, rise above all problems. Fly above it like a bird looking down on those anachronisms

EU heads the richest on earth but wants you poor so they make even more as immigration soars.

The new maid is humble and causes no trouble, the other one ran rampant telling all to the rabble.

Sin destroys decades of your life and if He's given you up to it you'll have no control/filled with strife.

In a post-Christian era female goddess religions emerge and lesbians become preachers.

LE FEMME and the Communist Spirit

GRIT the best determiner of life success: conscientiousness, dedication, tenacity, get er dun.

Decades of laborious failed attempts and embarrassing lessons then lift-off with God's blessin'

Your work is perfect tho' you aren't.

You can't teach an old dog new tricks so it took this to break thru the blockhead to bliss.

You could be a foulmouthed floozie for decades and didn't know it cuz it was a demon from Hades.

It was all demons and Jesus erases everything that occurred therein.

The churches have become wimped to adapt to the wimps in the pew who don't want the truth.

We're all sinners--we get caught up in things--but the point is repent then God and angels forget it.

"Low neuroticism" means freedom from negative emotions.

Relax, it was all a demon workin' thru you hon' and it's gone, irrelevant, non-applicable, NONE.

It's good them thinkin' you're dying then they'll leave you alone.

Although people cause trouble or joy, they still come and go so just seek God and on Him rely.

Stop resenting actors God created to teach you things. You learned em, they're gone: evil beings.

LE FEMME and the Communist Spirit

Evil is limitless, so horror opens you up to the dark abyss--a horrible pit you should wanna miss.

Lesson bringing wisdom and success: If you act right you'll be blessed/if you don't life's a mess.

I have often regretted my speech, never my silence. Xenocrates

Due to what Jesus did the past is literally erased and what a blessing and miracle on this day.

We get so high that old problems pale into insignificance--we've gone way beyond them since.

Justice, completion, victory.

Prepare to die, be a child--free of the phony/contrived and frantic deadlines, now be mild.

They get power over you thru intimidation, so if you have no fear (like Trump) how can they win?

I forgive you but can't see you cuz you're evil and it sears my soul.

Ingrown: just wanna be alone! Lock me in my room and throw away the key--that's the happiest place for me.

Don't plan your day just fall into the predetermined groove laid out for you (you still choose).

Oh well, just forget it all and look out the window. You've got a locked gate so they can't get to you.

Jesus came to divide families not to unite them, although it would be nice if they came along.

LE FEMME and the Communist Spirit

How to be heroic: refuse to go along with current narrative and state the truth to the barbaric.

Relish the opportunity to be an outsider cuz it's outsiders who change the world. Donald Trump

It's not really me it's God comin' thru. It's just what I do.

Treat the word "impossible" as nothing more than motivation. Donald Trump

Don't work today just savor and appreciate how far you've come and know you're almost done!

Don't rush to finish forcing the fit but wait to start so it completes itself so it's divinely perfect.

There's no lukewarm with God--He loves or He hates. We're told to hate sin so ok if you're that way.

People/generations die then there's no memory of you anyway so forget em and just be happy.

I hate most books. Long boring paragraphs not all inclusive short sentences which is all it took.

Genius has the capacity to say things simply, not a bunch of words to veil his lack of certainty.

People tend to repeat themselves, gesticulate, go too slow or bore us with unnecessary trivia.

Don't rush the end, completion itself is divine and patience (slow and steady) makes it fine.

Completion of Creative Act: a giant elaborate ceremony of inspiration and success so don't rush it.

LE FEMME and the Communist Spirit

Altho' IQ generally goes down with age for some it goes up- -the *Sage*.

It's not a matter of how much you've done just that *your time has come.*

Era of completion is here, I'm an inch away. But patience says: go easy, go slow, let God has His way.

It's so exciting to know God will complete everything you started. It's His thing, your co-Creator.

I'm waiting for that click in head to start the end. I haven't heard that click yet. Paul Newman

You mean you're so insignificant you don't warrant a platform? No, God has plans, get ready to go.

A book is a book--not like a building where you can see it but every page must be checked, darn it.

Make the books available--publish yourself--then totally rely on God to be your marketer/best sell.

I'm not here to sell books but to do what God told me to. It's my calling, that settles the issue.

One can never know when he will be done until that moment he's done. Thank you Albert Einstein

Just do what you do and suddenly be done.

You're done it's just a matter of *correct and firm* and you've won.

I know you're in a rush to finish but slow down a bit, you need the right frame of mind to be lit.

LE FEMME and the Communist Spirit

You're at your most powerful cuz you're most focused and that's cuz you're elders, confess it.

Your will not mine be done. You lead the way to complete and total world victory, then I've won.

The biggest failures come from finishing too soon. Wait for breakthrough but keep on low like stew.

Sure it's underground but there'll come a point where it all explodes and finally you're noticed.

They shake you up/censure by blocking "likes". Don't be bothered, keep posting, don't think twice.

A long succession of worthless accomplishments or one big creative act that took decades in fact?

They don't care if it took forty years they just think you're old. Transcend this generation/be bold.

There are no grey areas, it's black or white. Go by the book, wishy-washiness is a blight.

Don't worry cuz when the time comes to start you won't be able to not-start, pulled to the end.

Like a string in a sweater that unravels completely that's completion, then you are free.

Don't worry when it's time to start it's like a tidal wave completing itself naturally, so wait!

How to write. Lock em out, look out window, open mind.

Stop cowering. You're made in the image of God--strong, powerful--that's when He's behind it all.

LE FEMME and the Communist Spirit

You're in a new life and will never look back. Locked into a new dimension like white from black.

I feel like a rocket ready to take off.

Plant grows underground then suddenly sprouts--it is seen--and that's exactly how you will be.

Planted the seed then you waited--the biggest part of the journey--before God now rewards it.

I'm savoring the End of the Creative Act, like ocean going thru my veins/correct and firm, FIN.

Completion/retirement is like falling outa structure: our self-imposed urgent deadlines.

Celebrate your total world success tho' you're not done yet the final's locked into place, eh?

I know you want completion more than anything but don't rush the end--let God come in.

Here's the gist: God put talents in you for a specific job so hone those skills, give your twist.

World success transcends the weather, the place, current events or anything else: it's the ACE.

Success feels like an ocean going thru your veins.

You've done the work now relax and live off the fruits.

Prepare for world fame. Success overnight = renowned cuz you overcame all/fought the good fight.

LE FEMME and the Communist Spirit

Hippy

Main liberal shove-down: we're all equal, *ONE*.

The liberals you know are still ticked Trump's the boss and will never get over it/accept their loss.

Never accept someone's pronouns: that's the next level of insanity we must adapt to now.

Our president is beloved around the world so you're making fools of yourselves boys and girls.

Trump is a proud man: proud of himself, his achievements and his family--that's a good thing dummy.

Liberal cities are tolerant, politically correct, diversified and covered in needles, trash and feces.

They can't separate out the utopian image from what it *really* is--until it hits em in the face/DISSED.

Collectively mentally ill and there is no bottom to their evil, the contagion of madness in the people.

There's nothing they won't do, these kids. No more lines, like ISIS.

When states turn blue you have massive homeless problems too.

Liberal means you trash your city, allow anything goes, have sanctuary cities/ok citizen murder.

LE FEMME and the Communist Spirit

 Things got dirty in the 70's--we see debauched grandmommies justifying everything like trannies.

Political correctness is the mind virus of the left.

Just to be hip do you say bad things? Remember that to us clear minds, it's so embarrassing.

Distressed: It's astonishing to see just how much opposition there is from the anti-rational left.

It's brutal out here trying to get a message across facing brutality, de-platforming, banning.

The horrible names they call us to get the feral mob to attack us and to think it's CNN fake news.

To think that in my free country I can only move around with body guards protected from lib hordes.

Liberals move in mobs while conservatives are just themselves.

Since the liberal mob assembles (to do you in) you MUST have bodyguards, it's just astonishing.

If you really respect multi-opinions it should be no problem that we express em--but it is, isn't it.

People are offended by everything so why does it even matter save our free speech in tatters?

Donald Trump is the most pro-black president we've ever known. Darrell Scott

He's very direct, not like politicians going around and around in circles, all talk. Melania Trump

LE FEMME and the Communist Spirit

Liberals turn on a dime--flipping 180 in an hour, you know something else changed their mind.

If we give in to those taking offense soon we say nothing and less.

If it's an answer they don't like it's a "rant"

They monitor things "on behalf of the audience", how ridiculous with ramifications monstrous.

So the monitor censors in deference to the whole audience? It's tyrannical and I'm not having it.

"I'm asking you to be more respectful" means: curb your talk to what we want or be called awful.

Just censor the smut.

Open inquiry is basis of greatest civilization since best conclusions come after hearing ALL ideas.

Lauren Southern: How tenured hippies ruined everything.

Just cuz they live in their mother's basement, dependent, doesn't make em less dangerous.

California cares more about destigmatizing AIDs than they do about not spreading it/hate.

I'll never get over my fear of those boys—tho' now in their fifties it's seared in my history.

They hate normal people since normies wouldn't be into all their weird crap.

One thing about war: you demonize your enemy.

LE FEMME and the Communist Spirit

According to the crazy left enforcing federal law is the exact same thing as slavery.

The problem is old white people, they say. We just don't get their vision with hell to pay.

Not one scientist agrees you can determine your own gender just by saying so.

We're sick of catering to your trigger warning race/gender BS or safe spaces.

From their vantage point you're old but they're rude so don't go back/be happy/stay bold dude.

The saints said these people are crude and silly, so much superfluity.

If there's one sign of hope, it's this: ingratitude is the howl of hubris, and hubris comes before the fall. anonymous

Censorship FB/Twitter: You can't face your accusers, know why, nor prove them wrong--bummer.

Millennials more concerned with how they'll be viewed than with accuracy of their statements.

We don't wanna live in violent dysfunctional s**tholes infested by black and latin gang members.

Quitting Trump is their new platform--it isn't politics anymore it's the world's dumbest religion.

They wanna remove my only defense/protection not blame the shooters, the reason we need guns.

CNN represents the death of logic. CNN

Antifa-like resistance to all SCOTUS pix.

LE FEMME and the Communist Spirit

Liberal towns are quiet since everyone's afraid to speak but accepted narratives are ok to preach.

Signs to quit your school: Words like equity, diversity, inclusivity, white privilege, systemic racism.

They're not being educated but indoctrinated.

Contract is the basis of civilization for predictability in all our affairs but not to liberals, I declare.

Left is angry Tommy Robinson got out--the far right neo Nazi or whatever else they call the patriot.

Even smart men are a bit jealous of Trump from intrinsic envy of his SMV (sexual market value).

Academically suspect, ideologically possessed.

It's exhausting/debilitating to be in a cold-hearted relationship with those calling you a racist.

What Trump is doing for America is phenomenal and to that degree to liberals he's horrible.

The left is protected for everything it does. It's convinced everyone it's not the enemy, but it is.

Since self-restraint (saying NO) is a strength that's why weak men get into pornography I think.

Trump has radically expanded scholarships to minorities but the dems can't stand these victories.

Tolerance and universal love leads to acceptance of the occult.

Luciferian doctrine: tolerance, accept everything.

LE FEMME and the Communist Spirit

 2009: 60% of churchgoers voted for liberals. In other words, the baby killing and LGTB agendas.

You can't hate blacks but it's perfectly ok (politically correct) to hate whites.

Tolerance: "Do what thou wilt" is the whole law.

I believe in sin and can see how a church would be popular if it didn't.

They love Bianci's church cuz it won't mention sin just "inclusion"--same old slide into delusion.

Blacks fail from family breakdown/immorality but it's always called racism, that's their reality.

The mob is dumb and vain. Stefan Molyneux

They hate him so much you know he's for real.

Everything is relative, truth is nonexistent, utopia's within our reach: that is what they teach.

Why should utopians be happier than Christians? We have Almighty protecting, they have nothing.

There's nothing like telling truth to democrats and watching them go nuts. Jesse Lee Peterson

In the past, American blacks went to church on Sunday and dad was in the home disciplining.

Al Sharpton and Obama managed to divide the races more than anyone in the history of America.

You don't love your kids sending them to public schools or new scouts intending to destroy good.

135

LE FEMME and the Communist Spirit

This is the tyranny of consensus: everyone's afraid to speak in fear of the herd's punishment.

Only good sees evil but evil thinks it's all good can you believe it?

All they're doing by their stupidities is inoculating us against them finally.

Society is obsessed with speaking positively while afraid to speak truthfully = insanity.

They have nothing else but this lie about racism. To keep themselves together it nourishes em.

Such a sad way to live, adapting to the children of the lie--cave into radical agendas then die.

The black experience is hell but from their own behavior not from whites tho' that's what they tell.

When I look at the world it fills me with sorrow. Children today are gonna suffer tomorrow. Jesse

"Racism" is a made up word by race hustlers to keep blacks angry, resentful and controllable.

Even black preachers tout "racism" with the goal to indict whites and get more stuff from them.

The herd is like a flock of birds flying in perfect unison never questioning the flight pattern.

To disarm the people is the best and most effectual way to enslave them. George Mason

LE FEMME and the Communist Spirit

What Donald Trump is doing for America is phenomenal and to that degree to liberals he's horrible.

No army can stop an idea whose time has come. Victor Hugo

You can't prove things to people so never try to convince them you're not a racist, ever.

Animal farm: Everyone's equal but some are more equal than others.

Mesmerized by his looks and talent I was completely turned off when he opened his mouth.

Getting approval for leftwing activities or liberal viewpoints will make you increasingly outa joint.

So it's Trump's fault they came here illegally and are now being deported split from family?

Labeled our customs, culture/traditions as bigoted, intolerant, repressive and discriminatory.

A sign of a false person/preacher is saying all people are good.

100 year curse: Liberals prove themselves to be meanest most repugnant people on earth.

The herd works off each other's energy like a flock of birds assuming they're on course.

It's culture or sexual licentiousness, can't have both. Culture (like reputation) can vanish like smoke.

LE FEMME and the Communist Spirit

To veil evil doings they addict us to sex and trash until the moment too late/we don't want that.

They're redundant, take too much time, repeat or get pat, mediocre crummy platitudes/myths.

They hate Trump cuz hating white people is the trend but especially a patriarch worth billions.

Learn from Trump or be blue: Attack back, don't power down, don't worry what they say about you.

They obscure the doctrine of judgement cuz they don't want their sins judged, they love em.

Ever noticed how the most popular are twits?

Correct em and they say "you don't like me" cuz there's no right/wrong: it's called NEWSPEAK.

Trudeau blasting Trump after the deal is made? What poor character this little poser displayed.

Angry mobs have taken over London--sick of treachery like the imprisoning of Tommy Robinson.

Freedom of speech and self-defense are God-given human rights we're losing fast/last chance.

We're forced to self-censure to survive. Countries are falling into complete tyranny, no lie.

"Dignitarian harm" means: I have the right to act as I choose without disparaging remarks.

Censorship is about protecting the monopoly of liberalism and globalism in the public square.

LE FEMME and the Communist Spirit

Thanks Di Nero for showing us how ugly, unhinged, boorish, and boring Hollywood has become.

Like declining Rome, just when people are most evil we're called to be nice as we virtue signal.

We go from the age of betrayal to the age of straight shooting. Alex Jones

Di Nero must now rely on profane outbursts to be thrust into the public eye since his career died.

Early America was all Christian: helpful but until proof not trusting anyone.

First black president devastated the nation, abused the office and degraded the Whitehouse.

Don't talk to the enemy cuz he'll wear you out with debating insanity, false narratives and realities.

If you wanna make it in Hollywood just say "F--- TRUMP" that's it, cuz they're so intelligent.

They see traces of racism everywhere, they are "tracists". Dennis Miller

Liberal immaturity marked by Newspeak: your correction or criticism means "they don't like me"

Doublethink: All things are true even if in contradiction--a logical fallacy and why you're reactin'.

Ego never questions itself cuz it's Satan (come to steal, kill, destroy) whose actions are reflexive.

The college-brainwashed say it is all wrong but long before you were born we ALL got along.

LE FEMME and the Communist Spirit

Liberals don't wanna step on anyone's toes except those who know and say so.

They can never see it's a matter of principal. Principals aren't in their lexicon.

Taking life seriously and drawing lines they call being "nerved up".

That's establishing yourself as an artist putting out debauched crap like that? It won't last.

It's either personal attacks or triggering emotions like the current scam over border children.

A coward bows down to the enemy.

Obama the worst president ever don't put up a statue of him we don't ever wanna remember scum.

Lines are drawn/not safe to say anything hon'

An equal playing field means putting up with buffoons.

Dems are so immune to self-corrective critical thought truly they cannot see their absurdities.

Conservatives see good and evil while liberals see race. Jesse Lee Peterson

If you disagree with the racist narrative even with hard facts they'll instantly attack you back.

Nothing more dangerous than a lunatic mob and that's the reason for the second amendment.

LE FEMME and the Communist Spirit

Plan: Sell house in blue state, move to red state, start brand new life not bringing liberal sin/hate.

You think white racism is bad, black racism is thru the roof. Board up white people/tell the truth.

All angry people feel like victims and reflexively blame someone else for that, it's ridiculous.

Equal playing field tolerates buffoons.

Millions of American prisoners separated from their children and the left has never mentioned them.

Freaking out about non-American children at the border while butchering our own in the womb.

Millennials massively shifting to GOP. They're sick of forced conformity to this leftist crap/unfree.

The news isn't monolithic anymore, it 's channelized. It's two parallel universes, left vs. right.

The SJW mayors of cities and thus the police will take the side of Antifa in the war on the streets.

Walkaway movement has completely taken off. Who knew dumping the Democrats could be cool?

2 classes of people: coastal liberal elites and inland working poor--one is evil, the other we adore.

It's good Californians wanna get the hell out but please don't bring that crap here/we love God.

LE FEMME and the Communist Spirit

 Only after leaving a bad relationship (blue state) for a good one (red) do you realize how bad it was.

Coastal elites are evil that's why you're moving. Tho' liberals are affluent, doesn't mean a thing.

How to walk away: See headless liberal mob attack innocent people in an otherwise happy rally.

I moved to a red state and there were no adjustments save how "real" it all was, escaping scuzz.

We win on the war of ideas, they're so false they must rely on crybabies and bicycle locks.

700,000 homeless American kids and left won't lift a finger to help. Democrats, remove yourself.

Petulant over Hillary's loss they've launched a hate Trump campaign that is lethal and gross.

You can't hide the right. Tho' you don't talk politics to just get along, they know/avoid you on sight.

If you're right, decent, home-loving, patriotic and god-loving they will now hate your guts honey.

Better watch out because the left are petulant children but violent, outa control even the old.

Your art isn't about politics it's about your generation's narrative of such--old slogans outa touch.

In fact when you mimic this crap it's so embarrassing, up the wrong creek/thinking you're chic.

142

LE FEMME and the Communist Spirit

 A loving mother and strong father is at best unfashionable as the family is being dismantled.

Trump's reversing all of Obama's shrewdly crooked executive orders so be giddy for the future.

Taking on the herd hypnosis that everything goes, you go insane and there's nothing you know.

It's a mentality where virtue signaling reigns supreme cuz no one wants to be out of mainstream.

Having a relationship with media is like dating a woman who twists all you say/no win. Stefan

There's never enough for the left. Stefan Molyneux

The left is a collectivized mind, the right are individualists who don't group protest like dirty slime.

Morning news scene: They know nothing but say the right things, they're part of the team.

What's happened to the left? All they say is vile, disgusting, nauseating even from the best.

Late night comics are the highest paid traitors/brainwashers there are, groomed as big stars.

Late night comics are now just sanctimonious virtue signaling from the anti-Trump resistance.

Trudeau and leftists don't have answers to problems that aren't totally predictable ideologically.

143

LE FEMME and the Communist Spirit

 It takes a lifetime to develop your own theories otherwise you take on the current narrative/CRAZY.

They don't think, they run an ideology in their head and accept the output without question.

Liberal matrix blocks rational thought which is point by point adaptation to life, the whole lot.

Obama showed a disturbing but crystal-clear pattern of defending black racism towards white folks.

Trump didn't put kids in cages, Obama did that but even so it causes anti-Trump rages.

Why doesn't Joel Osteen discuss the devil, sin or hell? Cuz it's not nice and it sure wouldn't sell

HERETICS: Smiling preachers, yes-men, hell-deniers, globalists, all-is-one nuts/papal communists.

Beta male smiling preachers play both sides and "don't hate anybody" while truth can take a hike.

Wimpy churches don't tell the truth.

There are no "progressive preachers" cuz the Word is ageless applying to all times and spaces.

When people are killed they defend the thugs not the cops. They're calling good evil and evil good.

How can you be a man/woman of God and defend evil? That's what you're doing every day people.

LE FEMME and the Communist Spirit

Thank you Mr. Trump: a real man after being screwed by a communist who wanted us last in line.

Don't go down that alley into horror/porn, or decades in darkness blocked from life you'd adore.

Horror films are an entry point. These demons are no joke and you'll be irritated, tired, outa joint.

Speak up and be attacked or stay silent and warp your soul. Jordan Peterson

Millennials understood: Dictator killed millions = good. Offensive words = you're a no-good hood.

They don't wanna rip em from their mother's arms but ok to rip em from the womb, that's liberals.

What you're saying is not true though it seems so true cuz you're brainwashed thru and thru.

They weren't just wrong all these years but arrogant in their wrongness (our lives were a mess).

Jesus rebuked the sinner not groveling before him trying to be nice, that's just not so.

If they have perfect knowledge, why does the left fear/hate criticism?

Disputing the liberal stance has been heretical for decades. They'd get mad and we'd concede.

The churches have become wimped to adapt to the wimps in the pew who don't want the truth.

LE FEMME and the Communist Spirit

Obama massively expanded the police state. We all feared a knock at our door and felt desperate.

I would rather take a political risk in pursuit of peace than risk peace in pursuit of politics. Trump

Friends are "enlightened" going along with sin yet dirty/who knows where they've been?

Obama had a way of treating same sex marriage as if Jesus himself would approve/he was shrewd.

Trump is helping blacks more than any other president has.

The democrats have embraced violence by the mere fact Maxine Watters has not been silenced.

You may have power with the people, then you won't. Think about that when feeling arrogant.

They're socialist activists, not journalists.

It's hard to make people stop hating when they have invested their whole life in this tragedy.

I was thinking such dark things/vain imaginings and now it's all perfect/divine again, imagine that.

Forget acting ability, transgenders should get every role in Hollywood due to their sexual identity?

It's not where there's smoke there's fire when they're creating the narrative calling us liars.

To go out and beat up conservatives is their new way to make friends and socialize afterwards.

LE FEMME and the Communist Spirit

Civilization decay comes when the natural order is eliminated and all become degenerate.

While liberals are perpetually/professionally offended on behalf of others, the right is better.

Have faith we're winning the war tho' at the time it's hard losing jobs, family, income, whatever.

They keep going back to find dirt on him but he keeps moving forward/modern day Sansom.

If they get control and wipe out free speech we'll never again be able to get good men in like He.

CNN has lower ratings than the food network—ha ha condign punishment for those jerks.

America's the greatest country this side of heaven and we're losing it through complacency, nappin'

CNN doesn't report the news it fabricates it with fake parking lot scenes and we're all disgusted.

You don't go to heaven/avoid hell cuz you have talent ya know.

There's no such thing as racism, homophobism or sexism there's only good and evil, friends.

They made up words to control--so overcome it, love what's right and love God with all your might.

Anti-male Antifa are ruthless felons, perverts and lunatics armed to the teeth to destroy America.

LE FEMME and the Communist Spirit

 From their lowminds they jealously see him as a millionaire looking down on/telling em what to do.

The hip hop craze came over everyone thinking it's hip to be bad and now it's catastrophe/death.

I know you wanna kill em but be kind to diffuse the anger while stating boldly on all matters.

How dare you say you love your president. How dare you say meeting with Putin wasn't treason. Whoopi

In dense generations the intelligent aren't even nerds, just alien.

Art is to edify not to disgust/make us wanna die.

Trump could find a cure for cancer and they'd hate him for sure.

No matter what they'll never be chic--just don't have it, make wrong decisions, mentally effete.

Socialist lures: We'll fill your coffers even abort your kids ok just sit on your couch and vote as libs.

Cortez's views: socialist wrapped in ignorance. Cortez risk: Slash military and tax the rich.

Envy, theft, jealousy, covetousness, murder: that's socialism tho' its couched in sweet looks like her.

There's no such thing as good government, just limited or unlimited government.

All closed communities are the same: It's ok to lie to outsiders if it furthers their own game.

LE FEMME and the Communist Spirit

Unless you say you hate Trump you're not part of the club, that's Hollywood.

Obama showed a disturbing but crystal-clear pattern of defending black racism towards white folks.

Millennials understood: Dictator killed millions = good. Offensive words = you're a no-good hood.

They don't have it, cannot come up with it, a blank slate--mimicry/slogans was all they had of late.

Disputing the liberal stance has been heretical for decades. They'd get mad and we'd concede.

Left is aghast we'd ever question the unquestionable so get strong and stand against the rabble.

Brainwashed by a theory showing them as morally superior, of course they can't let it go sir.

They don't think, they run an ideology in their head and accept the output without question.

It's not only debauched it's low class and gross. Walk away gently, nip it in the bud/, be boss.

No depth, no originality yet they hang on to dead themes unthinkingly.

There is no "obvious consensus" against Trump just a mass brainwash and social hypnotic.

Propaganda is not news.

LE FEMME and the Communist Spirit

How can male feel good if his heritage is seen as repressive patriarchy? Left creates tragedy.

The normal competitive male drive is put down as tyrannical so how can he truly succeed or go on?

Take kids from school if hearing words "equity, inclusivity, white privilege or systemic racism"

Close school they're not being educated but indoctrinated and there's no excuse for it.

The left no longer considers us as fellow citizens but inferior or not even human. It's a war, amen.

They won't listen to facts, reason, logic or anything else disputing their views that we're all one.

I'm calling on God who is using Donald Trump. We can now see His plan to defeat the dumb.

Because we're in the right we're entirely spiritually connected: those are the patriots.

Riot is the voice of the unheard: Maxine Waters endorsing mob violence.

It's white privilege to call for civility. CNN

Trump has the power and courage of God within. It's so amazing to see it, America's best friend.

How can Trump have lunch with one who has just attacked him? Cuz he's not angry, it's nothing.

LE FEMME and the Communist Spirit

Before a liberal speaks he surveys the lay of the land, a good man speaks from heart without a plan.

Donald Trump has to tweet cuz the children of the lie (the media) block it so he must speak it.

Obama had full power of the state and he took that power and destroyed everything in his wake.

Run like you're going to lose or prepare to concede.

When Barrack Obama came in it pushed republicans far right and Cortez will do the same, alright?

Fake news needs a new Obama so they'll overlook her extreme views and the destruction too.

So moral clarity lies in programs that are completely untenable and will never be paid for?

To Cortez, Trump's an "authoritarian hyper-capitalist"

It's very easy to virtue signal about policies that have no impact as they're never implemented.

Trudeau's brave new world of freedom, equality, inclusivity makes many Canadians swing far right.

Taught to sin but smile. Cumbaya generation is bright colors hiding disgusting darkness so vile.

The biggest tax cuts in American history and they still hate him, what a mystery.

LE FEMME and the Communist Spirit

When in power they were kind/tolerant but lose power and their claws come out/they run amuck.

The America they envision is a curse. It was fantastic but they've made everything so much worse.

It was the democrats that interned the Japanese in WWII. Yes, weird despicables, it is you.

Out of liberal altruism you let everyone (and their mama) in and that's why you're not evolving.

Raised to be social they only feel comfortable surrounded by people but this is evil, just be real.

What ruined our hopes, dreams, lives? This social thing advanced in schools/filled with lies.

As usual Obama trashed our Founders from way back when and ditched our safety for left wing spin.

By Obama's abuse of certain laws he triggered social transformation without representation.

Ban the press dinner. The reprobate liberal mind is infinitely disgusting: depthless evil sinners.

Law and a godless moral code cannot protect us from evil. It's easier to ban guns from the people.

INFERIOR: Progressive underground/sixties sexual movement and anti-tradition counter culture.

God creates from nothing by the word of God alone, but they deny that making their own throne.

LE FEMME and the Communist Spirit

Schools took prayer out and sex in. Overnight America changed as God was replaced by Satan.

Brainwash, lose compass: Only God is stable: why we need the Highest.

Kids go to school and they can't think logically. Can't drill down, expound, learn--a cultural tragedy.

They want your children to turn em into an animal that hates God and disrespects you/the law.

To stick to the gospel gotta expound on what's happening so we can adapt to this thing.

Drudge: smut standup shocks DC--went way too far this time, you see.

It's easy to get hooked on the internet as they line up similar suggestions so you choose from it.

We are religious, the bible calls them sodomites so we call them sodomites. Russian Clergy

Trump's victory showed Russia there are two Americas but they only respect the conservatives.

I just love seeing the new nasty vile comics fall flat on their face. Ha ha what a total disgrace.

Left dressed up in tux/deluxe to celebrate bullying, vulgarity and hate and that's how the left wrecks.

The WHCD comedy standup was tasteless, aggressively unfunny and very sad. Laura Ingraham

LE FEMME and the Communist Spirit

 Weak are taken in by the flashy evil Hollywood creeps but God rewards the humble, His peeps.

A filthy comedian is but a reflection of hatred for tradition, Trump and decent Americans.

To the loving left Michelle Wolf was not vile. This is how they talk to each other, that's their style.

What they call comedy is now vile bullying. Tearing down nice people and all the while smiling.

They forgive without repentance over and again but then gossip all over town about them.

Forgiving without repentance creates murderers and it's done by little old ladies and fakers.

They forgive without repentance for the virtue signal dance then tell everyone and not by chance.

We're countering Obama who keeps saying "don't listen to them"

Pathological altruism: I will sell you my own children to avoid being called racist.

All cultures had slaves but Christians for shortest amount of time, treated them best and *ended it.*

They're cruel misjudgments held us down and took us back. We cowered in the face of this tactic.

Hardly anyone has the tools/facts to fight back. But I do and will give you ammunition against brats.

LE FEMME and the Communist Spirit

I am very excited about my new book except it puts me in a dangerous situation telling the truth.

This all comes down to one thing: liberals thinking everyone is alike. That's the blind--take a hike.

Childhood propaganda limits the practical implementation of adult rationality. Stefan Molyneux

I don't need anger management I need to be rid of the people making me angry.

IRAN nuclear wasn't a treaty just an Obama agreement that trump overturned and now ended.

Only strength is charismatic you'll never make it part of a weak-kneed, nightmarish catastrophe.

Be magnetic and charismatic by standing up against this s**t not by being one with these evil twits.

How cruel they are to call you a racist, an immoral label! Practice now: "I am NOT a racist"/turn the tables.

Profanity is such a cheap shot just to be accepted by the sluts and slobs. Be rare, choose God.

Cut em some slack they've been held way back by media hacks and Satan's schools of lax/no facts.

They simply don't know what they're talking about: virtue signalers for life and you can't go back.

They think they're saving you but it's communism in a nice image and not Christian, so bid adieu.

Watch your obscene gestures too. It's debased an entire generation and powerfully subliminal.

LE FEMME and the Communist Spirit

Aging baby boomers are the only thing holding the world together. When we die out, tragedy/horror.

It's a lost generation. They're lost cuz their grandparents were lost, the grossness is fixed.

It's almost like they speak another language, they're vulgar and illiterate but that's our kids.

Satan changes the image of God into his image and that explains the insanity you see at present.

Before you vote always ask if they approve of men going into girl's bathrooms. Cool fools.

When we fail God's able to instruct us. He that suffers has ceased from sin, the bible tells us.

I don't hate the youth it's what they've been taught, the problem is they ignore Jehovah God.

I don't hate the youth it's just how callous they've become. Think of the things they call fun!

I don't hate the youth it's just another realm altogether and they seem to want me gone, a dinosaur.

Calling us bigots: slogans/phrases you've learned by rote--can't think beyond lies you bought.

Us not dying out yet is the only thing keeping you from going over the edge /falling into sludge.

They programmed you thru your video games, what a bore you've become with nothing done.

LE FEMME and the Communist Spirit

I don't see how you can stand being around all those you call church, they've fallen away sir.

The popular church is demonic, a den of thieves encouraging sin and it's contagious/traumatic.

They look good, decent, rich, cool and high but without Jesus/repentance demons are rife.

Of course they love a church who won't mention sin just to be your friend, the sinner loves em.

I don't have to attend, I already know cuz it won't mention sin.

The mark of the true church is how many people don't come back.

There's a lot of racist gangs of black people and the epitome is Mad Dog Maxine Waters: evil.

Trump gave billions to black scholarships and still the madwoman Maxine Waters bitches.

Ireland joins throw-away community of irreplaceable human beings through abortion on demand.

Antifa: Failure to Launch Syndrome or afraid of not having shelter (mommy's home)?

It's culture or sexual licentiousness, you can't have both. Stefan Molyneux

The truth is outlawed. Free the truth-teller from the UK criminals.

Your problem was getting involved with em in the first place cuz if they never met you, you'd be ok.

LE FEMME and the Communist Spirit

This is a big social not a church, it would disgust and appall a (saintly) religious introvert.

Paul said no chattering in the church. The way you prattle in the sanctuary is irritating, a curse.

Bianci: what does she know, dressing like that and misleading children—a *religious* leader?

Outside forces have taken over churches as well as our country. It's a plan to kill religion/you/me.

If they knew who they were they'd be so bored with this! They must fill time or feel more lost.

Ireland was the last bastion of pro-life sentiment.

Nazi level tyranny: arresting those reporting on corruption then banning anyone telling about it.

Blacks want justice for everything but what about the whites who died to end slavery? Nothing

We react to demons in em, children of the lie call that racism but that all dissolves once we know em.

When slogans trump logic, we've reached the end and can't debate it--so just get to safety.

It's not racism they are judging evil: demons. It wasn't that way, they were well accepted not lemons.

It's not racism, they are judging evil: demons. It wasn't that way, they were well accepted not lemons.

LE FEMME and the Communist Spirit

Kids won't learn critical thinking unless given both sides of the argument and they don't get that.

It's not tolerance, love or feel-good but about social deconstruction--destroying our world.

It's not about feelings, they're exploiting your feelings as a billy club against our civilization.

It brings us to tears: them glorifying the destruction of social norms for thousands of years.

People are horrible so don't expect any better and you won't be disappointed.

Today we mourn those who died so we remain unharmed.

Bring on the authoritarianism, it's only bolstering and corroborating populist sentiments!

For race and sex equalists politics is personal. It's how they see themselves, just can't get real.

White Europeans like Shakespeare are now universal but native symbols are appropriation, cultural.

It's a blend of socialism and false Christianity.

So many call themselves Christians but are not.

If you don't read the news you're uninformed. If you read the news you're misinformed. Stefan Molyneux

Everyone is a racist and they don't even know it. That's their spiel and we're darn sick of it.

LE FEMME and the Communist Spirit

 When progressives win they impose weird stuff on ya. Real reality is natural but not in America.

Roseanne's better off, the show woulda turned: open borders Islamic crap, social justice warrior stuff.

Starbach's reeducation close: Virtue signaling by Soros who's behind it all.

Roseanne fallout shows why you never apologize to the left. And so maudlin-- that part I don't get.

To the extent their art is social justice type stuff Trump's victories only reveal their fluff.

Obama and Hillary shut down whole towns. Fredonia devastated next to me, all mines gone.

Their whole world was turned upside down, the ontologically fatal insight that they've lost ground.

Neo-liberal thought virus running rampant thru our culture: do not engage with "I'm not a racist".

The second you start to beg and prove your valor or virtue ("I'm not a racist") you've lost it.

When Roseanne met em half way she lost our support--apologizing to left is not like a victor.

We have a right to put people down/hurt feelings with our speech--they do, ten times worse ok.

The African American liberal always gets a pass, Roseanne does not even though she apologized.

LE FEMME and the Communist Spirit

To a conservative it seems everyone is liberal or calls themselves conservative but not actual.

It's not about Roseanne but the double standard taking over the land: we can't speak but they can.

This isn't Christianity it's communism with virtue signaling.

He who departs from evil makes himself a prey and it's lack of justice that displeases God today.

Donald Trump is not a racist but a realist and a greenist: he wants prosperity for all of us.

Trash the 2nd amendment cuz we can't have armed pop and tyrannical government at the same time.

After the FOXES were dominant there's a return to the LION beginning with Donald Trump.

Academic Jihad: Rewriting history and reality, making everyone angry, inciting cultural suicide.

Miseducated/dangerous thinking--lawfare, litigation jihad: they don't like what you said, you've had it.

In fear of being sued, they shut up. No, not you but everyone else in terror will no longer talk.

When it comes to emotions/feelings they ignore the facts and logic has nothing to do with it.

White people love feeling good about themselves by feeling bad about being white. Jarad Taylor

LE FEMME and the Communist Spirit

They move on you, take your privacy/solitude, demand you take others in (you've got room): REFUSE.

Donald Trump: the Great White Hope.

Equalize everything: male and female, and all races, are the same. Charming differences, gone.

Putin likes the ladies. He's not a soy boy, girlie man, buggery or silly tranny.

University is a free flow of ideas not safe spaces and deplatforming those with whom you disagree.

Censorship in academia is stifled truth in the name of feelings.

You say we're not destroyed? Look at our schools, look at California or Detroit, invasions overnight.

Us dinosaurs will be outa here and it'll all implode cuz you guys know nothing what Jesus spoke.

WHO were the ones who moved, enslaved or killed the American Indians? Democrats: Jacksonians.

Democrats took Indian land/gave it to white settlers in exchange for votes--it's always the rats, no?

One group of Americans (Dems) did terrible things and another group (Reps) stopped them.

Demo Frisco spends 30 million a year cleaning up fecal matter, needles and trash--it's so liberal!

"Equal and equitable outcome" means to debase whites cuz our IQ explains success out of sight.

LE FEMME and the Communist Spirit

Modern art is coupled with sophistic explanations--that's ridiculous as it should stand on its own.

Wordy explanations of art means it's incomplete, didn't do it's job, picking up where you left off.

Did Michelangelo give explanations of his paintings or do they just stand on their own, scintillating?

You need wordy explanations of your art because it's so dull, ineffectual and nondescript?

Black men are whining like little girls about white people holding them back. Jesse Peterson

Black people are suffering--their men not worth a dime--due to family break down/moral slide.

I ask you where you're going and you tell me where you've been. Please answer the question.

Youth don't have maturity/brain power to see thru scams so hold your head up high/just ignore em.

Insane crazy brainwashed kids actually want open borders and say racism exists so I say: be rid.

Feel pity (despite fear of violence) for these crazy kids who can't think and push you to the brink.

Dumb kids not aware/don't care how illegals destroy black jobs, slaughter animals or kill our pets.

Kids have suffered such a cramdown of insanity I say: round em all up and bring em back to reality.

LE FEMME and the Communist Spirit

You subvert an organization by putting people in it who don't belong there.

Groups like Boy Scouts fail when they have a particular political viewpoint, not desire for success.

The thing about the left is that in nothing flat they turn the good guys into the bad just like that.

Most blacks (98%) literally hate white Americans but it wasn't that way before. Jesse Peterson

The many black preachers talking against whites from the pulpit are no good. Jesse Peterson

In the past blacks had two parent families, were religious and would discuss bible verses.

There was no racism and black men didn't whine about persecution and we were friends then.

They could dance and Soul Train ruled! Tall and thin not chunky burly scary mean debauched fools.

Grew up without fathers/family then Barrack tells em it's the white man's fault and they're angry.

The blacks are not free thinkers anymore and don't believe in principals or values, family or God.

It's gotten so bad we expect blacks to act that way and cater to them or be called racist: high pay.

Not your imagination tho' they'll say it is. You're scared of something/don't need to know what it is.

LE FEMME and the Communist Spirit

It's not about your color or whether male or female but the God you serve. Jesse Lee Peterson

Catalyst: They've been spoiled thru free stuff while leaders tell em whites (Trump) are racist.

Liberal media/dems tell em it's all about race not what's right, repeating same mistakes/no light.

Worst disaster ever: No father/being raised by liberal mothers yet liberals see that as utopia.

Blacks call evil good--they love it. Like "This is America" the reflection of darkness and the crooked.

They hate good and love "This is America" video--more than anything else this shows evil agenda.

Blacks: destruction of the family, loss of fathers, hatred of mothers and blaming it all on whites.

Because they're so angry they love entertainment which drives conflict but triggers feeling dissed.

The video was so spiritually dark and they love this stuff. Think of that, liberals can't get enough.

Don't ever fear them because they have no courage just a false sense of intimidation/evil-loving.

Think black: all the same way, dumbed down, demoralized, persecution complex, acting like fools.

They will never get better as long as teachers, parents, preachers allow em to blame others.

LE FEMME and the Communist Spirit

 Anger brings despair and despair kills the soul. Life becomes dark, meaningless, mean, old.

Normal people don't defend murderers but the democrats defend MS-13--what, for potential voters?

Same creepy politicians against calling murderous thugs "animals" are ok with abortion of children.

Instead of God and devil they call it "positive/negative power": no punishments/rewards.

Obama divided us, weakened the nation, taxes/regulations, took away jobs, opened borders = CHAOS.

Why would the left be defending the country's most violent street gang? Not delusional, lunatic.

After defending MS-13 murderers the left blames NRA for Santa Fe Shooting: how inferior.

I marveled at the royal wedding Christian when the UK is filling in with the opposite orientation.

Homosexuality's not about love, family or civil rights--it's about sex and anger blocking repentance.

Transgender suicide rate: 87% and you think it's great?

80 million millennials so brainwashed they fall for this crap

Donald Trump is not a girlie man and that's why they hate him.

Whites with highest grades are rejected for the wrong skin color.

Blacks are more violent/rapacious but it's pinned on whites who just live their own lives.

LE FEMME and the Communist Spirit

Causation: A combination of being insane and extremely low self-esteem in a toxic nation.

He's a straight, white, Christian, conservative man of POWER--hated by those without fathers.

Good man recognizes evil calling it "animal" while left says "they're all good" confusing the people.

That's why we love Trump: he sees it, says it and nails it while liberals never see a difference.

If it's all good would left see Hitler as good? They never answer questions or we're misunderstood.

"Animal": Only the good can see/nail evil while evil says it's all good except conservative people.

Using "animals" to describe em doesn't even begin to peg these horrific hellish gang members.

Yak-yak-yak, blah-blah-blah, all social hypnotism and accepted narratives, what a bore you are.

It's good Meghan can cook but what of the liberal feminist stuff she's spouting like a kook?

Meghan Markle the Queen of Diversity giving feminist speeches but with the old queens she clashes.

What is conservative, really? God-given rights, limited government, personal responsibility.

He's fifth in line so why not split from royal duty to jet-set with Hollywood, and good riddance.

LE FEMME and the Communist Spirit

Modernity is debauchery, clear and simple. It's advanced thru platitudes and vagueries, puerile.

I don't blame the Queen for hating the stuff she's hearing, I'd hate it too if it were in my family.

It's almost like it's planned: a half black pretty feminist spouting the lines we hate the most.

You wanna ban guns? Gun-free London is the murder capital of the world using knives, what fun.

If all gun owners are responsible for those gun crimes then all men are responsible for rapes.

Reflected Glory: Blacks *all* married to royalty. Did same thing with Obummer: *all* of em were president.

Unlike a fine wine the Obamas become more disgusting with time--got PTSD from all the lyin'.

You see, I remember how blacks used to be and that is why I am so disgusted with thee.

Told they can't be racist, they get worse. Get ready white America black racism thru the roof.

Identity politics took colleges but also hard sciences--technology, math, engineering: imagine that.

Identity politics: the results will be disastrous for American innovation and competitiveness.

How to attract graduate level students: No one's left behind as we simply lower standards.

LE FEMME and the Communist Spirit

What you call "sexually experienced" is just a lack of impulse-control: a slut.

Past Christians broke away from a decaying world so sinful but they don't think that way now.

Rather than setting aside the world and being stoic, churches are like going to a rock concert.

Modern Christianity: Don't question anything I do I just wanna feel good about myself.

National Science Foundation (NSF) is consumed by diversity ideology: it's the biggest mystery?

Identity politics: how science is taught/qualifications evaluated and the results are disastrous.

Evil liberals like Markle put the ideals of social justice ahead of the interests of the people.

Michelle Obama lives off spoils of his position taking more than given saying she deserves em.

SJW isn't even a nerd just going along with the herd by virtue signaling and adolescent anger.

You don't seem intelligent to be doing these angry, edgy "art" diatribes of these SJW tribes.

1984: the past was erased, the erasure was forgotten and the lie became the truth. Stefan Molyneux

All over the country they say "blacks and Hispanics can't follow the rules so ditch the rules."

LE FEMME and the Communist Spirit

 We're under attack. They've gotten Ireland to kill all their babies now it's one big abortion mill.

We've been led like lambs to the slaughter--this any asinine fool can see, they just wanted voters.

It's a bell shaped curve of the HERD to which most adapt and love but the saints are separate = HOLY.

Catholics are great folks but evil's taken it over.

Even in schools they're banning the word "Jesus" cuz it's a dirty word that hurts people's feelings.

Don't blame it on poverty. People were broke in the depression but weren't thugs out robbing.

Facebook, twitter and the other dopamine manipulators know that the web's depressing us.

Don't forget the protestors of 1776 were Brits! Ha ha the stoic Brit is really nice until he isn't.

At last, UK citizens climbing the fences at 10 Downing Street!

Harvey Weinstein was a Hillary and Obama supporter.

Watching underage images (feeling shame cuz it stinks), end up in jail quicker than they think.

Porn addict: "Always looking for greater buzz leading to a darker place you never believed possible".

They're self-medicating with porn and each time need a greater hardcore hit—more and more.

LE FEMME and the Communist Spirit

 Meeting old friends again is unproductive because they're all liberals and I'm a conservative.

UK judges trying to ban steak knives--it's never enough for lefties.

It used to be Christians were hardliners against the occult but now even churchgoers don't know.

All liberal labels like homophobia, transphobia or Islamaphobia translates to: "let me speak"

They must shut down the argument in case they lose it knowing it's built on sand. Melanie Phillips

Postmodernism means there is no such thing as objective truth.

They don't conclude from evidence, they conclude first then just force the fit with the facts.

Church lady took in 5 young boys/never blamed em for a thing and they went to prison, no kidding.

You're angry cuz mom was mad & you had an absent dad but you should be unemotional/a man.

Don't reflect mom's anger cuz that's feminine tho' it makes us shudder. Be a man/poise of a ruler.

Men never used to cry, can you believe that? The family relied on his stability/none were fat.

Sin disfigures people. Blacks used to be godly/beautiful but now NOT due to no-dad, sin and evil.

Blacks in the sixties were familial, beautiful, responsible and spiritual. Now it's the opposite, no?

LE FEMME and the Communist Spirit

There is no racism, only SIN. This is all contrived to get us fightin' so they can take over/our guns.

It's constructive anger: if we gotta fight we will. The problem is going along with the swill.

The white man is not the problem it's the way children are being raised, the little hellions.

The wicked call the gospel "flat earth" but wait till they die they'll see they're under a curse.

Justin Trudeau has never uttered a syllable that was not a gross platitude of stupidity. Gareth Rydal

It's legal but dam is it a bug so please shut up.

News never tells truth cuz they don't know it, don't want you to know it or been told not to say it.

Many stars sign a blood contract to get famous but later they're taken out when it fits the agenda.

Though they brag these liberals don't care about you they're economic hit men for the globalists.

Our dear leader is too much: He just keeps on winning yet liberals hate him saying he's sinning.

Trudeau is weak and dishonest: a limp handshake, can't trust him, will turn when he gets the chance.

LE FEMME and the Communist Spirit

Little boy attacking big daddy? Oh man I'm glued to the tube this is too much, so historic/shady.

Justin was weak & mild during talks then after Trump left mocked strong: "won't be pushed around".

Little wimp Trudeau's childish play has massive far-reaching consequences starting that day.

Little man Justin stabbed Trump in the back as he walked out the door. Tragic, embarrassing, deplorable.

Trudeau's political stunt was the worst political calculation of Canadian history. Peter Navarro

Trump fixed everything then after he left Trudeau pulls a weak treacherous stunt behind his back.

Trudeau threw a torpedo after they agreed--what a betrayal and so weak and immature, ya know.

Trudeau's bad faith diplomacy with Trump then stabbing him in the back publicly: how wimpy.

Fair Trade is now to be called Fool Trade if it is not Reciprocal. Donald Trump

Kim can't see American weakness so Trump must strike back hard as the POTUS thank goodness.

Di Nero said "F Trump" and anyone in the audience who cheered will now have a career slump.

LE FEMME and the Communist Spirit

Stunt press conference after the king left. How immature, how low after Trump went so far.

The conservative media like The Blaze have the same owners as the left--wake up about fakes.

Since the 70's good were hated and didn't know why, but then isolation/porn = soul died.

Seeing genders means I'm transphobic.

Admiring man and wife is homophobic.

Those into dignitarian harm have no problem ill-dignifying us on the right, I've often been alarmed.

Trudeau acted meekly while he was there then backstabbed after Trump left and they defend this?

CNN loves Trudeau only cuz the enemy of their enemy is their friend, just like brats or children.

Little man Justin couldn't resist sniping at Trump after he left and liberals see it as greatness?

Trump had every right to push back against this amateur political stunt of Trudeau the grunt.

Now we even Like Kim better than Justin.

Fake news knows nothing of politics. Bad faith diplomacy is a big deal and Justin Trudeau did it.

LE FEMME and the Communist Spirit

It takes President Trump's leadership to succeed where others haven't. Kellyanne Conway

People are intimidated by the true man though in movies they admire the fearless men in Bonanza.

Because he was grandstanding he couldn't see what he was doing. Trump will win, Trudeau is failing.

Look at the R-E-S-P-E-C-T Trump gets all over the world. They respect strength unlike us, fooled.

Trudeau made ass of himself in India so tried to regain in polls by taking on strong man of America.

UK has become an evil land where pedophiles walk free but those reporting on em are in prison.

Most powerful country in the world doesn't have to play nice and whether loved or loathed/no matter.

All that matters is they learn it doesn't benefit em to have disagreements with you, the hegemon'

Trump is so far ahead we couldn't possibly calculate his thinking. TV news arrogantly wrong/stinking.

A gang of boys held her hostage in her own house and cops wouldn't step in due to the ACLU!

From their lowminds they jealously see him as a millionaire looking down on/telling em what to do.

LE FEMME and the Communist Spirit

The Trudeau-Trump thing has got me so enthralled. It's about good vs. bad character, wow.

A debauched tone came over everybody it was 1990 and it was trendy to be sinful and shady.

Homeschooling protects kids from violence and Marxism. Ron Paul

Why go outa your way to look ridiculous just to be part of a club of the foolish?

It's quality over quantity, forget the masses. Tho' it's great if to God you bring in the most I guess.

The amazing and brilliant Trump video that swung the deal with Kim Jun Un and made him heel.

So to mitigate against sex crime you put out more indecent stuff bad as second hand cussing.

Trump is unburdened by the truth said the ultimate liars: CNN News. CNN

"Any president could have done this" fake news said in another dis while they lose ratings fast.

Art of the Deal in North Korea: You're either gonna die in poverty or be rich with great prosperity.

Once a precedent is set for something it's nothing later to make a mental leap and be wrong.

Hollywood elites worship Alister Crowley who killed his own son in a ritual: these are awful people.

LE FEMME and the Communist Spirit

True manhood is strong foundation--honesty, trust, health and sound mind not anger/whining.

Whether your art is lasting or not all depends on your premise and that's liberal or conservative.

To get the correct views from cable news you must invert everything they say. Tucker Carlson

Bashing Trump for enforcing laws he didn't even sign off on, the horrible legacy/leavings of Obama.

Pedophilia is being normalized by liberal media.

It's always about what's good for them not what's right. The solution is to get clear/seek His might.

No angry person can see. They see intellectually but that's a false way of seeing. Jesse Lee Peterson

Kleptos can't help stealing cuz their father is the stealing killing destroying lying conniving devil.

They start the ritual with an anal rape then a demon enters in and that's your beloved Hollywood.

Once you forgive you can see and life is no problem at all.

Forgive em cuz they can't help themselves.

PTSD: going crazy only when finally in safety.

LE FEMME and the Communist Spirit

 Liberals are posers, they're not real. Studies show they're ten times more likely to steal.

You can't be a Democrat and a child of God cuz it's anti-God, anti-family and anti-unborn child.

The Democrats are godless as well: anti-truth, anti-America and anti-everything good/opposing hell.

Even if they make more money with a family film they wanna "shatter taboos"/push boundaries.

Racism doesn't exist: problem is spiritual, straight outa single parent home. Jesse Lee Peterson

Liberals learn Trump is blamed for children Obama put in cages, quieting the people's rages.

97% black people voted for the democratic party and Obama twice--and you say they're nice?

Rachel Maddow cries: All drama, all lies.

In NYC more black babies aborted than born but liberals only care about babies on the border.

As soon as they had an edge they took everything no matter what we said but God gave us a hedge.

Satan always quotes the bible for you. Test fruits

They're children of the lie, not God's kids. Otherwise how could they ever believe this s--t?

LE FEMME and the Communist Spirit

It's man over woman and this other thing is disgustin'

Must tell the truth or children of the lie will take your country.

They spend all their time on social media and don't know how to be men.

Blacks suffering due to lack of moral character and destruction of family but are told it's you/me.

Mockers at feasts or wherever we get together. Learn about the leech then tell the world: speak.

Don't try to convince them cuz the children of the lie won't hear, they're blinded by a demon spirit.

Black immorality due to destruction of the family and lack of character blamed on white culture.

Laura Bush and the RINOS are the same as Hillary and the Democrats so don't kid yourselves.

But now blacks don't have intact families and it's all gone to hell overnight, a liberal blight.

They blame it on slavery 200 years ago rather than the failure of the parents young and old.

Blacks weren't raping and robbing stores because they had morals and knew what was right.

A growing pattern of intimidation, public embarrassment and mob scenes against Republican officials.

Stores and players suffer horribly with their public leftist stance and so will Red Hen Restaurants.

LE FEMME and the Communist Spirit

Because Christianity makes you want to do what is right not wrong it is hated by the evil throng.

Liberal's house not built on a strong foundation but sand--this the commie children can't understand.

It's not just a "difference of opinion" but inability to discern good vs. evil or right from wrong.

A lunatic mob is an atom bomb and this broad is inciting restaurant blowups? Black/woman/slob

We don't like you anymore not cuz of your skin color but how you act, justify and demand more.

They will lose a civil war so quickly, but let them start it. Mike Adams

Be honest with them but not angry with them, they literally can't help it. Jesse Lee Peterson

Kids may have common sense but so messed up by their liberal parents they doubt themselves.

Once you decide the people who disagree with you are Nazis everything is allowed/potentially awful.

Stop telling me how good and great you are when I only see petty pilfering by sticky fingers.

Barrack Obama nearly destroyed this country cuz people were afraid to tell the truth even me.

Obama was the worst: far left, liberal, godless redistribution of wealth black liberation socialist

LE FEMME and the Communist Spirit

Evil democratic party is anti-unborn child/family/God in public square, anti-military, pro-sodomy.

Blacks in 60's loved God, respected what was right and worked hard, restrained from doing bad.

They're already reprobate if they can't see God in the heavens or political leaven.

The conflate. Taking black violence and averaging it in, saying "America is violence and doom".

Liberals believe blacks are only in prison from racism not criminality so they're released early.

Knockout games--killing old white people. Black cowards are never mentioned now, what evil.

The enormous number of blacks in prison means: "whites are doing it too but not arrested", see?

I love your city, I love your restaurants, but I'm never coming back. San Francisco visitor

Since God gave the gift of artistic/intellectual discernment let Him decide on those varmints.

The left are trained by opinion leaders how to spot you right away and it's from what you say.

Don't you dare give em a break cuz they hate children thru abortion/giving pedophiles a platform.

Though Antifa has been media-fomented to vicious violence they'll still be responsible for it.

LE FEMME and the Communist Spirit

Every time you mimic/follow a herd narrative you make a fool of yourself. Neurosis = brainwash.

No way is this a lost cause. We take our power back and it's game over and they've lost.

Pornography is a doorway, it's about brain chemicals that hook the guy.

Now it's coming out through paid contributors on CNN with great regularity that we're Nazis.

With the system-is-rigged mentality you quit after one failure then same cycle for your future.

Fraudulent social justice brings empathy burnout.

They make a big fanfare only to dissolve to vapor cuz their work is a bummer and you're better.

Pay attention fanbase: They accuse the children of God of doing what they're doing, always.

Don't get emotionally involved with liberals, that's how they control you. Avoid emotion/stay logic.

If they say filthy things they're filthy liberals and avoid them like the plague but stay cordial.

Trump's gotten so much done despite fighting with RINO republicans, media/democrat scum.

She's known as Crazy Maxine/Mad Maxine so I wouldn't worry she'll be gone/we'll be free.

182

LE FEMME and the Communist Spirit

Media has lost all its moral authority and what mattered most: their ability to move and shape us.

At this point you will find out who's with God and who isn't. Those who say it's all God ain't fishin'

We take authority over the shedding of innocent blood and debauchery thick across the land.

Trudeau: male feminist caught in a grope. Watch the drama teacher get outa this one, the dope.

Raise your black power fist, it won't put one dime in your pocket or make one good friend.

Black power is no power, what we need is the power of God. Jesse Lee Peterson

While interrupting constantly they accuse you of micro-aggressing already.

May you make millions acting like this but I predict short life cuz it's ridiculous/God's all there is.

God works thru the prayers of His saints.

Arrested in Canada for preaching the gospel.

Smiling all the time is not what this is all about! Life is serious, do His work and be sober.

They refuse to judge as it may "hurt" the person, we *must* judge sin and hate it for good reason.

Smiling preachers wanna be everyone's friend but to the clear they're just phony and sickening.

183

LE FEMME and the Communist Spirit

 Instead of hating these crazy people just realize they need parenting and to repent of evil.

If you're not gonna use the bible (the word) in your churches throw the bible outa your churches.

They go to church dressed as harlots and thugs.

If you're a white in Philly you're always ready for unpredicted racial violence. Colin Flaherty

To remedy black-on-white violence you first have to face it but is it ever admitted? Not a chance

They write long boring paragraphs of stuff I don't need to know--no one knows the quintessential.

Ha ha whatever they shine a light on to put us down just makes people more aware of scum.

Never stop speaking cuz they're too dumb to get it--it's for the future when they've woke to it.

Left thinks they've perfect knowledge so should be immune from criticism, so watch out m'am.

Left is aghast we'd ever question the unquestionable so get strong and stand against the rabble.

Not all, not all, not all...but MOST. Jesse Lee Peterson

We are not allowed to talk that way but fortunately our president LOVES to/says it's all-ok.

LE FEMME and the Communist Spirit

We just wanna live our lives like everyone else. No one's thinking how to mess blacks up.

These people can do wrong while the good guy's put away. Innocent men jailed for being white, ok?

It's skin color above truth. They portray thugs as innocent children and we see this in Europe too.

Racism doesn't exist. Blacks are in a fallen state listening to liars who get them angry and pist.

We cross the street when they appear not because of their color but fear cuz they're violent dear.

Brainwashed by a theory showing them as morally superior, of course they can't let it go sir.

They've hijacked Christianity to make it into what they want it to be and approve of their insanity.

The left isn't opposed to Kavanaugh it's the constitution they're scared of.

The only way they can feel important is to resort to violence or they will trigger it themselves.

The only solution to liberal laws is homeschool or solid church school unlearning to be cool.

Blacks weren't acting this way (bad) when they had parents but the government wrecked all this.

Democrats/liberals have personal agendas while using black people for personal gain in America

LE FEMME and the Communist Spirit

 Lying to people, keeping them angry. That's how they do it and it's a terrible distortion of reality.

When people don't have God on their side they use words like "racism" to control you/don't let em.

We must fight this battle with truth, it has nothing to do with color folks. Jesse Lee Peterson

Blacks were betrayed by father/mother--no one else--then triggered/angered by hustlers of race.

Blacks have not made progress, they've regressed back and it's a real mess.

77% of black babies are born out of wedlock and that's highly moral and from good stock?

So the first black president indicates progress? He was the worst ever and the country regressed.

Never put up statue of Obama cuz we don't want to ever remember nor think of him in America.

Why is Trump a racist now but awarded for helping blacks back then? It's all about the money hon'

Trump blimp or pathetic party balloon?

The greatest time in America when evil is exposed like never before and Trump says "want more?"

They get angry right away due to the shock but later say wow that was great, I won't block.

LE FEMME and the Communist Spirit

Even preachers/pastors spout that crap: new age pagan religion about we're all "one" as fact.

My "friends" used it as a platform to bigot against me. I hated AA/Al Anon: it's the herd/liberal.

They're all liberals by default because it's all they're taught even in the churches, imagine that.

We just wanna live our lives like everyone else. No one's thinking how to mess up blacks.

Mental revolutions occur suddenly in a mass realignment to a new beat.

These Revitalization Movements have occurred all through history, led by a charismatic leader.

The left is boring, only truth is energizing. Bold words: truth and energy vs. silly tangents: sleepy.

Lawless in their application of their laws cuz it's all about foolish ideas stuck in their craws.

Liberal men are afraid of guns--our one right and rare privilege ensuring life is happy, safe, fun.

Life is no more fun in times of war or break-in by ruffians. In an instant it changes so get your guns.

Just when I think I'm immune to their attacks they hit me again but I'm gonna win this thing.

Since each victory strengthens em no one's safe from their attacks. Most families, liberals in fact.

LE FEMME and the Communist Spirit

Liberal social clubs are about rewarding the false positive image, it's a lie and a fake Mrs.

Hate speech is just a made-up term for tyranny and censorship.

They said I didn't wanna get well cuz I hated very boring AA meetings filled with virtue signaling.

They attack us cuz they haven't anything else. No debate, data, facts, logic or history to tell.

Turning affluent neighborhoods blue makes everyone blue and the liberals finally feel screwed.

AA is not my therapy if it's a liberal social club.

It's now a pro-Trump page so if you don't like him kindly leave so a smart one takes your place.

There is no "obvious consensus" against Trump just a mass brainwash and social hypnotic.

Even Fox is going against Trump. Meanwhile they're shadow-banning harmless Diamond and Silk.

While driving us away they're driving the mainstream left's political activists into political apathy.

They're creating a system that will further isolate coastal elites (like uber drivers refusing us a seat).

Liberals please leave, to make room for others more able and willing to learn truth as God sees it.

LE FEMME and the Communist Spirit

Leftist cities/police defending people who attack women and children: I've experienced this friends.

"News" used to be reporting actual news. Now it's sitting around in a discussion without a clue.

Christian gospel songs now banned from facebook and our holidays now banned by Apple crooks.

Not only do they wanna break America's back but also teach us a lesson: not just lose but hurtin'.

They hate conservative blacks so they've now banned the sweet Diamond and Silk: facts!

Our boys are going out against these Antifa creeps--our American spirit is now running the streets.

It's only blue cities that allow this Antifa violence and the police are in on it-- it's been admitted.

Trump, please: report em to FBI, get task force against Antifa and stand up for your supporters!

Obama tried to start race wars, knowing cop killings were justified but not saying it (LIARS).

Find the local chapter of ProudBoys and know fifty of you can handle 1000 of those violent guys.

60% of kids in public schools are "minorities" and now the white kids are cowering in a tragedy.

LE FEMME and the Communist Spirit

Godly can't be afraid of words cuz the children of the lie use em having no power, only curse.

If liberals can't intimidate you with words or threats they have nothing and will disappear/all wet.

You will make us strong, you'll feed US, cowards. We didn't start the fight but we'll finish it, scum.

Don't vote for politicians just cuz they're black cuz they'll sell you down the Maxine Waters, fact.

They always make two mistakes rather than admit to one. David Knight

240 million crowd together in urban areas and it's growing, feel sorry for ya.

Frisco mayor won't negate public defecators.

Left: Once one starts doing it they all start up--like the restaurant thing or The View broads.

Main cosmology shovedown since kindergarden: we're all ONE (equal) and thus this violence hon'.

Why would you ever go on this knock-down drag-out lunatic show The View?

They've a predetermined narrative comfortable in that studio with a liberal audience: The View.

They can't stand the fact you have real substantive answers or that you've done your homework.

"Everyone knows that" no everyone does not know that, what seems obvious is full of crap.

LE FEMME and the Communist Spirit

 It's quite different being a big fish in a little pond to being in a bigger pond facing the sharks.

Your vanity's stoked by being a big fish in a small pond but once upstream you face the mob.

They hate him like a fervent jilted lover bent on revenge. Why do they hate Donald Trump I ask?

Free market increases foe's sexual market value and they can't stand that so the fight is genetic.

Censorship in academia is stifled truth in the name of feelings.

75% of the time the established power goes to outright war with the rising one.

If your pastor says something that contradicts the Book why have it at all? Just throw it in the trash.

Engrained in Marxism is envy, so in social generations solitude is the only way to stay free

Why they hate him: It's all about SMV (Sexual Market Value) of Donald Trump bringing hateful envy.

A billionaire has SMV and it's ok if he's black or liberal but a conservative white man that ends it all.

Thinking you're right and not allowing debate is fascism whether from right or the left, same.

Economy is soaring, ISIS defeated, tax cuts for everyone, finally protection but they HATE him.

LE FEMME and the Communist Spirit

 People are intimidated by real man Trump tho' in movies they admire the fearless men in Bonanza.

Trump is so far ahead we couldn't possibly calculate his thinking. TV news arrogantly wrong/stinking.

Liberals are uninformed, scientifically vacuous and dangerous wanting post-birth abortions.

Democrats ruin every city they run cuz they're globalists: debauched and evil not homespun.

Why go outa your way to look ridiculous just to be part of a club of the foolish?

It's a lot harder to crowd their space and sexually harass people these days, Bill Clinton says.

Trump is unburdened by the truth said the ultimate liars: CNN News.

"Any president could have done this" fake news said in another dis while they lose ratings fast.

I want these criminals stopped, I want these traitors out of our country, I want em off our back!

Half of democrat higher ups wanna have sex with kids. Alex Jones

They've gone collectively mentally ill and they have no bottom/infinitely evil.

Living in a media bubble they don't know what's goin' on.

Have nothing to do with evil and it's a sliding variable but they've gone into full blown illness, mental.

Is this normal, or am I in a bad part of town? San Francisco visitor

LE FEMME and the Communist Spirit

To be on the left you have to be hostile to whites, men and heteronormativity so be smart/walk away.

If you preachers don't mention sin let alone hell, how will they know/why would they repent y'all?

The things imposed on us now as everything's breaking loose and there are no lines/SWINE.

Movies are insults to our intelligence: not appropriate for children but too childish for adults.

Silly movies are too much for children to understand but not enough to challenge an adult mind.

We've gotten so used to censorship we accept it but don't: it's criminal, racketeering, discriminating.

We watched our words in fear of their abuse if it was different from the matrix they learned.

Trudeau and leftists don't have answers to problems that aren't totally predictable ideologically.

It's easy for the world to seduce your kids when they see you as hypocrites.

Trump didn't put kids in cages, Obama did that but even so it causes anti-Trump rages.

Why do I say they're immoral? 75% illegitimate births, a no-brainer.

Where did they ever get the notion that this is ok? It's gone way too far into evil, just walk away.

CNN pays for TVs/cable for schools: they brainwash you first then have you write papers on it, how cool.

LE FEMME and the Communist Spirit

Liberals are horrible saying kill babies and old people.

The youth are so low hanging on, you know dude, shallow SJW morals and values.

It's Holy Hatred and it's ok to be shaken up and get others to face it too--we've been silenced too long.

We now see that by banning together we can beat you, defund you and make our voice heard.

With sinners in control life becomes boring, uncharming and reckless like Frisco's public defecators.

Those who think it's a predestined groove work all day. Those who say "free will" fritter it away.

Hollywood movies distract us while we're robbed blind/dumbed down by the very same criminals.

I know you wanna kill em but be kind to diffuse the anger while stating boldly on all matters.

Guard mind/eyes cuz once you see it it's etched, unforgettable, horrible and a means to stumble.

Zuck Facebook lost 100 billion cuz we're sick of em and all their censorin'

Donald offered one mil to Pocahontus to prove she's Indian and she won't do it/course we knew it.

Dumb as box of rocks going along with social hypnotics and now can't walk it back/you don't rock.

Evil has a lure--that is temptation, we all have to overcome it.

LE FEMME and the Communist Spirit

 While the left gets away with murder the right gets the PC guillotine with the slightest infractions.

"Racism" is a made-up word to intimidate white people/dumb down people of color, both suckers.

They lynch straight white married rich men of great power.

The more they go after the president the more his supporters come close/we know the best.

Childhood propaganda limits the practical implementation of adult rationality. Stefan Molyneux

Facebook is a meeting of the minds of people who think like you or who you can convince to.

Telling blacks to fear whites: Blacks are 93% more likely to be killed by a black man in a fight.

Democrats are for workers but put em outa work.

Roundtable discussion with an obvious agenda, that's the news (CNN, NBC) and we're sick of ya!

Stand against the incompetence/intransigence of the corporate globalist media--time to arrest!

Don't plan on speaking boldly for it's gotten dangerous must now proceed with caution: WARNING.

Propaganda is not news.

LE FEMME and the Communist Spirit

"Hate speech" is a made-up word by those in power to create division and eventually take over.

Liberals are too dumb to know the difference between "some" and "all"--it's low IQ y'all.

Don't adapt to your kids lower level just so you won't be alone. Be a beacon and teach morals.

Just cuz a lesbian has grandchildren doesn't mean the issue is settled, read the good book, ma'am.

The left promotes pedophilia now, so if we speak out against child rape that's hate speech?

Now that Alex is gone the revolution has begun. Silent no more, it's as bad as Tommy Robinson.

Oh sorry, I shouldn't have said that, someone will make a big deal out of it-- aren't we sick of this?

As we're being banned they jump on the bandwagon cuz they're so weak/have nothing goin'.

The anti-white racism is becoming dangerous and ominous for the future, have caution please.

After Alex was banned we all just left and the whole thing folded. It left a horrible taste, moldy.

Today's left assumes automatically that a brown person is victimized by a white in authority. START

Truth is hate for those who hate the truth.

They want chaos cuz they're not in power--that's the rule they follow so better prepare y'all.

LE FEMME and the Communist Spirit

Commie

Picturestrip described how we got here,
total masochists giving our country away.
True meritocracy is color/gender blind but they
don't want that, it's all they have on their mind.

Commie

Those who despise themselves will

LE FEMME and the Communist Spirit

be despised by others. Alex Gulland

The immigrant flood will continue year after year until it is stopped.

Kindness to strangers is cruelty to your own children. Europe will wake up or die, brethren.

"Western Chauvinism" is: an exuberant love and appreciation for everything the west is.

A nation is people, people are a nation. When you bring in strange cultures all the greatness is gone.

Calling us xenophobic cuz we want just our own is an insult.

We don't owe our country to rest of the world.

They simply assert it: "Diversity is our strength", end of argument.

The democrats love immigration due to false compassion and the desire to win elections.

If they're globalists in the way they govern they're making a mint and their income is doublin'

But sorry, nationalism is now contagious and mainstream.

White Christian men are the most hated species on earth. Never cower, stand against the curse.

Majority of whites are good people but we've been fed this lie that they are hateful and evil.
Former FLOTUS Michelle Obama: The root of all problems is "the white man". Go away crazy woman.

Marxists want open borders--they despise Christian culture and know barbarians would crush her.

We don't want em here!

LE FEMME and the Communist Spirit

They care nothing for border children just their own power and will use any argument to get there.

The stakes could not be higher, we're talking about America.

The biggest, stupidest and most dangerous 21st century myth: "Diversity is our greatest strength".

Just as the whites have most diversity they are also hated more than anytime in their history.

Conservatives are the only relief from the prevailing mind-numbing orthodoxy of racial diversity.

Diversity is a failed social experiment imposed upon innocent peoples which is possibly insoluble.

To them It's got to be done, our destiny: to feed on each other's differences and make history.

CENSORSHIP AND WITCH HUNTS

They're gonna make it work, forcing the fit. They won't stop until we're all dead thru a failed myth.

The media acts as though the demographic drivers of this crisis are nonexistent: RIP CNN.

The problem is immorality, family breakdown and mass immigration from antithetical societies not racism.

Conflict is between white boomers who worked for pensions and POCs dependent on handouts.
The dumb ingrates storm our land demanding our treasures and deference so stand up, man.

Brute strangers rob us blind, destroy our social fabric then demand we accept their predations.

80% of the women crossing the border get raped but when Trump called em rapists fems hate it.

LE FEMME and the Communist Spirit

Criminals are scared and desperate cuz they know the mean, stinking reality of globalism is evident.

The foes are like Bill Clinton: Ran as populist but governed as globalist. Be watchmen or be pist.

You ought to be careful with your society for in a minute it could be swept away from thee.

Globalism makes all borders irrelevant.

Accepting more invaders is the road to hell for Europe. Czech PM

For thousands of years immigrants adapted to the host but now the host must adapt to immigrants.

Since globalization is transcultural, states must adapt to immigration "make em welcome".

They wanna go home anyway so pull the plug and they'll leave, vamoose, disappear, hurray!

All across Europe is a revitalization of classical greatness as well as what Christianity really means.

Fake news is trying to destroy America and are the friends of our enemies the globalists, you betcha.

Politicians protect guilty for votes and police are so afraid of being branded racist you know.

Multiculturalists accept stoning for raped women. You accept all cultures, right, vermin?

Barrack knew exactly what he was doing destroying America for he's not a dumb man just barbaric.

Venezuelan socialism: Water, water everywhere but not a drop to drink.

LE FEMME and the Communist Spirit

Shunned from the center we got stronger on the periphery as we worked on ourselves and waited.

Europe is being invaded and they are allowing it to happen. We are next unless a quick turnaround.

Arrest Merkel.
Help individual refugees, yes. But floods coming here, no thanks!

Virtue signaling and feeling good about herself is more important than possibly millions killed.

Such jubilation--what are they fleeing from? Not having to work--they've been promised millions.

We don't believe the argument anymore that mass migration is needed due to emergency. Viktor Orban

Italy's new populist government's euroskepticism has alarmed Brussels, good we don't need em.

The Renaissance and the Enlightenment were derived from Christian European culture in sum.

It's not about left vs. right but left vs. west.

No wonder leftist politicians applaud whites becoming a minority in their own country.

Leftist ideology is based on equality of outcome not equality of opportunity= Communism/unfree.

Society that puts equality ahead of freedom will end up with neither but put freedom first, *both*.

"Inequality is evil" so different outcomes can *only* mean something unjust has happened?

I know what it's like people moving in on you and whether town or block it's hell on earth too.

LE FEMME and the Communist Spirit

We just want our own lives or there's weird stuff happening, outa control, exasperating.

Parallel societies, political Islam and radicalization have no place in our country. Sebastian Kurz

All across Europe they're reversing the demographic decline by having babies, lots of em, oh my.

Conservative traditionalists are having children while liberal globalists aren't so it's turning around.

Spain will wake up but a huge price to pay as these incompatible people cause trouble, ok?

Spain, there's only one solution: they gotta go back!

The pathological altruism of immature kids says "we need more migrants" feeling so sorry for em.

MERKEL MADNESS AND FEMALE ILLOGIC/VIRTUE SIGNALING

"We need new blood to fund pensions" but they go right on the dole, taxpayers fund em.

Anyone who hasn't come into contact with em has no idea what they're like, esp. those from Africa.

Red carpet glamour after spouting fibbers without suffering consequences of open borders.

They seem fresh and innovative but their ideas are destructive and old, socialism is cold.

Innocent German people were punished twice: once by Hitler then Merkel and her open borders.

Merkel, the Chancellor of Open Borders has embraced the evil policies of the far-left dreamers.

LE FEMME and the Communist Spirit

Crazy socialist Merkel let a flood into small bucolic towns. Preposterous, evil, shut her down!

Her two experiments--open borders and green energy--enriched her friends with halos immense.

"We need new blood to fund pensions" but they go right on the dole, taxpayers fund em.

"No more power without accountability--you've met your match in Donald Trump" Nigel Farage

Mrs. Mae we did not vote for a transition but to instantly leave the EU organization. Nigel Farage

BBC has been encrypted into the globalist cause so we're down on them too as fake news.

When Europeans realize a picture of dead child doesn't mean to destroy their societies, Soros dies.

For Hitler it was an ideological crusade worth the sacrifice of millions of lives and it's similar today.

The whole world should be able to come here supported by you and anything less is racism.

ICE: Those who enforce the law are criminals and the real criminals are new American citizens?

War is peace, freedom is slavery, ignorance is strength. George Orwell

Today if you don't want immigrants flooding your country you are racist by default/you're kicked out.

It's "IN" to be poor/austere cuz the globalists want you under their thumb, it's called Feudalism.

EU heads the richest on earth but wants you poor so they make even more as immigration soars.

LE FEMME and the Communist Spirit

It's a military invasion disguised as a migrant refugee crisis so gear up/get ready.

When the facts make blacks or Hispanics look bad you don't say it--now you know the facts.

No sane country lets millions of foreigners in to put their snouts in the public trough. Jarad Taylor

When enough people get angry things change.

As illegals pile up on the border the dems insist on letting em all along with those who keep comin'.

Unskilled, uncultured, unwanted. Liberals wanna change all that and make em top of the pack.

The nasty EU stands for "tolerance, diversity and human rights" and we are rejecting them all.

Matteo Salvini knows they're trying to flood Europe with illegal migrants funded by troublemakers.

Low IQ pops propagate the spread of infectious diseases.

We're on path of South Africa with irrevocable snowball of black on white violence, God help us.

Whites are the most accepting/tolerant in the world. No other race accepts floods of foreigners.

Cultures vary on callousness vs. sensitivity. Whites always escape when non-whites rule visibly.

Kill whitey race baiting is now merging with Islam and gangster culture, all socially engineered.

Diversity means: fewer white people. How could anyone celebrate their declining influence?

LE FEMME and the Communist Spirit

Whites letting others become a dominant force in their country is a virtuous and good thing?

They come in boats: low IQ pops. To the white men they say: "shut up, pay the bills and die off".

An unarmed invasion brings the same as an armed one: loss of land, language, culture, mind.

We don't want foreigners waltzing into our country and going on the public dole. Jared Taylor

The entire mission of the children of the lie is to lower the percentage of whites in our country.

The people they're bringing in are socialist, communist, without values and used to s-holes.

When people of color take over America it's done, over.

Look at the violence, the lack of respect, the nastiness, the dirtiness and ghettos brought to us.

White Americans created the greatest country this side of heaven and now look at Europe, it's gone.

White people in Europe don't have the freedom to disagree with the people of color, the POCs.

White people built Europe and now POCs are there destroying it/arresting em for speaking up

The whites joined forces in America after the awful shock of the nasty evil communist Obama.

After they saw what nasty Barrack did to this great country in just 8 years they said NEVER AGAIN.

After that disaster they brought in a good man, a white man, a straight conservative Christian.

LE FEMME and the Communist Spirit

POCs are not happy that the whites organized and outvoted em for the good of the country.

Creeps like Maxine Waters are hellbent on bringing in POCs as they hate the Great White Hope.

Dems want these godless people here not cuz they love em but for the votes.

They seduce these pops with free stuff and setting them up to hate white people enough.

Anomalies: white authors writing "unbearable whiteness"--self-hatred you never see in other races.

It's genetic with whites to just subsume guilt and assume the whole world's problems. Gavin Mcinnes

Equal rights is vastly different from "equality of outcome" which is deadly and dangerous.

We want borders/see immigrants as the problem, they want immigrants, borders are the problem.

They're taught by way of apps and leaflets how to lie when they get here and move us all out.

Logic: Can't take care of both immigrants AND citizens and Salvini's answered that contradiction.

With illegal immigration they're shown by way of apps how to beat the system to our disadvantage.

The more immigration the less tolerance. Diversity does not increase it as the liberals insist.

One man's death is a tragedy but a million is just a statistic. Stalin

White people must have their own homeland or it's the end.

Communist countries see American gayness as a plot to bring them down. Careful, see all around.

LE FEMME and the Communist Spirit

Victory: Long jail sentence for worldwide nationalist populist overturned, time for great cheer!

Tommy Robinson is now a right-wing martyr and the left is really pist about losing that place sir.

Martyr freed/revolution has begun!

We're joining with other countries against globalist dehumanizing dynamics and tendencies.

The new trend in Latin America is an abrupt turn to the right and it's nationalism/God almighty.

Why isn't Maxine Waters, Jesse Jackson or the NACP talking about the black genocide in L.A.?

The race hustlers are allowing the obvious black genocide in L.A. to happen for the votes alone.

We're no more a country standing for your demented words of violence and death. Be cautious! Trump

A group can suffer setbacks but as long as it has it's territorial space it can recover.

Champagne socialists push diversity to please the youth while not having to live with the poop.

The effects of multiculturalism are ethnic and cultural displacement.

Throwing acid in one's face with goal of disfigurement is a foreign and barbaric practice.

Merkel madness is about to topple and I'm so glad she's been murderously awful for her people.

How does evil Soros get his political gain? My overseeing Europe's "managed decline".

LE FEMME and the Communist Spirit

Throwing Tommy Robinson into prison population is like throwing a baby to the shark's ocean.

The indigent masses want what you have and that's the BIG DRAW of these socialist candidates.

Socialism appeals to the dumb/low IQ pops who can't learn from history and want your yachts.

Trump is pulling the biggest sting in history.

Democrats have always been socialist--gimme free stuff--they're just now making their move.

If whites don't have babies they'll soon be a minority as their country becomes a ghetto surely.

Europe's decline is rapid and terminal.

Far from being grateful migrants despise Germans.

We're to gladly self-destruct with our first interests global despite what we have to swallow? Hell no.

Political correctness blocked discussion of similarities or differences between groups of people.

Horrible agenda 21 Plan: All the earth's billions of inhabitants will inhabit only 41 megacities.

Stop blaming or resenting interlopers and put the focus back on you for allowing open borders.
The anti-Brexit anti-Trump liberals gave us the determination to succeed and we finally are now.

Being bred out of existence is white genocide.

The biggest thing to em is unequal outcomes: If it's not equal we did something to block em.

LE FEMME and the Communist Spirit

Every society: Renaissance (blooming phase) then corruption, decadence, weirdness, pyramids.

You know you live in a great country when people who detest it refuse to leave. Candace Owens

They are communists: they wanna take everything from you and give it to others or themselves.

This is simply horrible. They're killing pets, they're raping everything. God help us soon I pray!

Their arguments have become increasingly sophomoric and opaque as whites are blamed/hated.

The bigger our wall against reality/the less consequences to treachery the less we keep out enemies.

Pope washes feet of a wishy washy internationalist view of Islam.

Just pull the plug they'll self-deport

Works like a top: accused of racism, we pay up.

Tyranny comes in a happy face.

Remain independent of the vicissitudes of demographic change with a fence and locked gate.

Send them back or they'll keep coming.

Only house/fence/locked gate remains impervious to the vicissitudes of demographic change.
Political Islam is parallel societies and radical tendencies.

Elites want post-industrial austerity with world poverty and a tiny elite tax exempt/diplomatic immunity.

People are waking up all over the world, elections throwing globalists and IMF World Bank Out.

LE FEMME and the Communist Spirit

Patriots in the UK don't wanna be ruled by Transylvanian aristocracy or wicca like Theresa Mae.

How is the white man bad if his religion is mocked but he doesn't kill anyone/just sad? END

The only people you're allowed to hate are white.

Whereas it used to be natural to defend borders of a nation now that's nativist, xenophobic, bigoted.

What they used to do with swords they now do with immigrant conquerors.

We lost our defenses when told "they're all good" and to be welcoming to the depraved dunces.

What scares me is Sharia Law and their hatred of dogs.

The effects of multiculturalism are ethnic and cultural displacement.

Freaks me out man. The way they treat animals, that's the barometer of a good/humane culture.

We're going into a very dark time. Thank God I'll be gone but we're seeing the Beginning of the End.

Give white man a pile of bricks/he'll build a city, give black man a city/he'll build a pile of bricks.

"Race is not a biological construct but a social one" Liberal scientist, insane and dumb.

Liberal myth we hate: We are all the same so should just relax and enjoy giving our country away.

America not Babylon but Nineveh.

Despite the obviousness of failed policies the left is compelled to try em again: insanity.

You evil Hungarians dare to want to preserve your own culture. EU stance

LE FEMME and the Communist Spirit

Salvini to connect all nationalist parties in Europe to seal the deal--the new direction rid of Merkel.

Well done Matteo Salvini my friend I'd love to buy you a drink sometime or even champagne.

I have felt like the underdog HELPLESS as the foreign invasion goes on without cessation.

They played to the soundbite: "abolish ice"

Who knew that helping the poor could make you so rich.

There's no way for government to make us better, all it can do is make us worse. Derek Hunter

A rising tide raises all boats but a sinking tide sinks em all too just look at Venezuela you fools.

Stop having babies to save resources but then import half the third world to make up for it.

Liberals have proven illegal aliens are more important than citizens or our children who need help.

All white people just have to die. Oprah Winfrey

The white man freed the slaves--and lost life and limbs to do it--but still they are always blamed.

Buckle up folks, somethin' huge is comin'
We love our pets--cats and dogs--but these third world pops hate em or neglect em, it's bad man.

What would happen if millions of foreigners marched into Pakistan? Maybe now you can understand.

Using child separation to open us up/destroy our borders--not a word re: children of prisoners.

LE FEMME and the Communist Spirit

Left hates Trump cuz they hate prosperity. They want us all poor/dumbed down to accept tyranny.

Whites are the most accepting/tolerant in the world. No other race accepts floods of foreigners.

Whites went from tolerance to weakness, afraid to stand up to invasion, abuse and meanness.

We Americans are very nice till we're not--we're quickly reaching that point so buddy watch out.

Why on earth would you let all these strangers into your house? The whole world's laughing at us.

Real men would be lined up on the border, not let em in to suck off the public trough/intruders.

Told not to discriminate whites don't prefer their race over another but it's very different all over.

At first they're too ashamed to be a patriot. But later when it's accepted they joyfully do it.

Classic Trump: equilibrium disruption, resolution. Drop bomb then say "I love Theresa Mae".

Making em adapt to us is like we're "superior" cuz all races are alike says the liberal (inferior).

CNN and all fake news is globalist and that's why they hate America-first president, a nationalist.
Modern democracies are committed to diversity but then things don't work and we're all unhappy.

Despite nation's average IQ there are those who shoot through higher/not offended or angered.

Increasingly nations are defending unique culture and traditions against this globalist hegemon.

LE FEMME and the Communist Spirit

To MAGA we gotta spread it to the world by being on the side of nationalism for all, forever.

As Obama was a closer to globalist disaster Trump is ENDING the secular One World Order.

Why we love him, the modern day Sansom: he's the Great White Hope saving all the nations.

Trump: Immigration is politically destabilizing the entire country in this national emergency.

They're bringing the mess, the s-hole societies, to our country. Donald Trump

If you love your nation/race you argue against diversity and I've already explained this travesty.

If someone calls you a bigot turn off the spigot or never see em again, the idiots.

CNN globalists want us taken over and destroyed.

White people usually have only tiny families now, no match for a thousand cousins all around.

Every culture's different in set up. Things like interpersonal distance, reaction time, frame ups.

Let's not talk about labels just the free stuff I'm going to give everyone. Alexandria Cortez

Socialists are always bread and circus free stuff then take everything you have and more you nut.

He's a communist but really just a villain.

Mad Mother Merkel guaranteed there would be NO LIMITS on money migrants entering Germany.

Whites went from tolerance to weakness, afraid to stand up to invasion, abuse and meanness.

LE FEMME and the Communist Spirit

Seven acid attacks a day in London and we know where that came from but can't say it or prison.

They have an agenda: dispossessing those of white European descent from their birthright.

It's how they treat dogs and cats too--everything is strange, harsh, brutish.

Stop pushing white guilt and making white students feel less than others.

Multiculturalism and diversity are just anti-white policies.

Christianity is about mercy not the harsh punishments of the East.

The new groups flooding in will have an edge due to their nepotism, identitarianism and tribalism.

"We don't want all these people here" said everyone all throughout Europe to Soro's deaf ears.

Our piece of the pie is much smaller or we'll be banished altogether and you want open borders?

When country becomes prosperous they wanna take your money to buy groups, so stay on top of it.

Listen to the race hustler who runs away, always blaming it on slavery not the absent family.

It's unreported, understand that! You don't know the extent black on white slaughter/it's a fact.

Freedom State means sanctuary state.

As whites we gotta be forted against Muslims but also blacks out to get us if we love Trump/facts.

Non-whites aren't having anti-your-people propaganda pushed on em so they can be proud.

LE FEMME and the Communist Spirit

For the entire border little children are used as subway tokens to get into America/fraud, scam.

POC's (people of color) are knockin' em out (whites all over) and it's unreported (study deeper).

Pedophilia in migrant camps: It's when you keep the kids together with adults that this happens.

Cortez wants to eliminate ICE and the protector of your sovereignty, the constitution—yikes.

Shrieking liberals are advocating burning ICE down and several offices are under siege now.

Ms. cortez wants to ban guns *and* open the borders completely: prepare for mass slaughter lady.

Well paid globalist pawns: Late night comics don't have talent like Johnny Carson, come on.

Anyone for open borders hates blacks, whites, women, kids and pets.

Taught stupidity and feelings are all that matters so 40% of kids want socialism like Sanders.

Is it jealousy re: income inequality? Seeking to make the rich poor not the poor to have more.

Economic warfare makes countries poor to control em, tho' globalists dying it's still happening.

Socialists will fight you for the crumbs on your table so it's all about "free stuff" not these labels.

Extremist open border democrats make me sick cuz they don't think of us putting up with this.

White South Africans can't live on their own soil but blacks can claim all of Europe, that's all.

LE FEMME and the Communist Spirit

If Europe doesn't welcome millions of impoverished low IQ men in, it will be ruined. EU saying

99% of the inventions that we take for granted were by white men, that hunted/targeted vermin.

They want news taken down cuz for most of us the idea of being replaced is too much to fathom.

They are majority minority cities.

What a great thing, our cities are flooded with CEOs, doctors, lawyers and other immigrants.

As long as the new majority conforms to us it will be fine, but we know that won't happen anytime.

More ethnic diversity = more conflict and segregation.

A black is 20x, an Hispanic 8x more likely to attack a white than visa versa but this info is censored.

Americanism not globalism is our credo. What we want is victory for the world. Donald Trump

Everywhere we look border walls are going up, not coming down. Celebrate nationalism.

Democrats are going for hyper-globalist open borders just when the world is rejecting this horror.

Ms. open-borders Cortez is triggering such a swing to the right, HA HA it's happening overnight.

Our value system stands 100% opposed to everything they stand for so they don't assimilate ever.

Demographic path to liberal control of USA.

Democrats don't care about children, illegal or American. Jesse Lee Peterson

LE FEMME and the Communist Spirit

It's a false outrage, folks. They don't care about children (look at all the abortions) but votes.

Masochism is also the communist spirit. Not only take mine but give away gifts from ancestors.

We have nothing in common except we're both human beings. Every thing they curse, I believe.

You and I are split, poles apart--nothing whatsoever in common, for a start.

Elite Plan: Make culture deteriorate to be controllable.

Like the Fabian socialists they slowly develop the new mind and it's hell on earth, cruel/unkind.

College gives right attitude towards minorities and means to live as far away as possible. Jared Taylor

Self-righteous politicians chant mantra of integration while living in gated communities/protection.

Not an ounce of sympathy for whites being displaced by non-whites seen as bigots, a blight.

"Integration is our goal" but not for me or my children. --Most politicians

A cobweb of watch groups needed for diversity-maintenance--cuz it's unnatural and we hate it.

Free of government, communities are racially homogeneous: churches, families, clubs, happiness.

Nothing could be more obvious: diversity of tribe/religion means violence, hatred and derision.

It's not just school brainwash cramdown it's also the inset cosmology "we are all one" insanity.

Why isn't diversity good for Mexico? You mean they wouldn't want to be reduced to minorities so low?

LE FEMME and the Communist Spirit

Could Mexico be tricked to think it's "cultural enrichment" if we took over their country/government?

Mexicans are more clever than wimpy whites—they'd recognize an invasion of their rights.

Racial Diversity is a one-way issue. Only whites are expected to give what is theirs to you.

Ultimate insult: demand whites celebrate diversity—their capitulation, lost influence and country.

Whites built successful desirable societies and desperate non-whites want badly to live in them.

We demand Mexico open their borders, let us buy land and vote down there just like they do here.

Multiracialism is a suicidal fad and elite globalist set-up that's bad: we've been had.

In the face of dispossession whites are too paralyzed to resist so they succumb.

Race Realism is so simple and so obvious: the races vary in temperament and intelligence.
It's not racism to not want your grandkid black or when the neighborhood changes to move: fact.

Different outcomes due to different abilities not prejudice but in America they're taught to hate us.

Kids should be taught about race in the fifth grade but they're taught it doesn't exist instead.

If we live in two different worlds psychologically there's no way we can share a space physically.

We are the first civilization in history to give up what is ours then search for a place to go, darn.

LE FEMME and the Communist Spirit

Whites are giving up what was theirs and marching off the stage of history: unprecedented, truly.

Self-destructive insanity (of whites being displaced from their country) is new to our species.

Blacks commit a disproportionate amount of crime (statistics from Dept. of Justice and FBI).

They WANT blacks and whites fighting so they can make new laws and take control instantly.

Racism has never existed but is being used to incite riots, take control and kill resistance.

Thousands of whites killed by blacks every day but police investigate the "N" word on Le Bron's gate.

Instead of being angry at crazy kids just see they bought the whole scam and ALL of it's points.

Illegal aliens now named "illegal permanent residents"

Illegals are destroying black community with jobs, crime and health care but liberals don't care.

Since 1965 USA has seen the largest invasion in human history: 61 million is a CATASTROPHE.

The alt-right is against one group dominating another so this mass immigration is a fetter.

The Alt-Right are just race realists (of the obvious) but are always called white supremacists.

Lead you into sin so we all fall down then they take control of everything around.

The Luciferian spirit is anti-God, anti-Christ and anti-you and it's goal is complete and total control.

LE FEMME and the Communist Spirit

He/she is demon possessed to ever push an agenda like that

New cause with electoral prospects: illegal aliens while American poor people get lip service.

Globalists' plan: Islamify the entire world.

Demographics is destiny and oh what a tragedy.

In nations or homes, prosperity is followed by decadence as walls come down/inflow of immigrants.

Obama said rural towns were "too white" so brought in third world pops to vote/dominate overnight.

Greece prohibits protests against having your town invaded/trashed in collusion with Islamofascists.

"Riots, vehicular attacks, priest beheadings or honor killings aren't linked to migration" -Macron/dumb

France, Germany: 80% are on the dole. Deport them or it's suicide from dysfunction/murderous souls.

Islam linking with green and communist movements to vote everyone's rights away despite disparity.
World War III begins with demographic leftist globalist directives voting all our rights away.

Macron/Merkel take marching orders from same source of course, not just dumb creating the worst.

They're dominating/raping women everywhere and the police do nothing in Paris, Berlin, London.

It's always been the same: kill the men and rape/enslave the women and that's what's happening.

The crusades were a defense against multi-century Islamic invasions of Europe.

LE FEMME and the Communist Spirit

Their goal was to conquer Europe and was being achieved then they fought back, a defensive war.

They celebrate this history and say that's the goal: take over again.

They took away your culture. Without a culture you're intimidated and submit to their tyranny.

Whites are blamed for slavery when they ended it and all cultures had slaves/blacks most of it.

European castles: the defense against Muslim slaveholders until quite recently in history.

For whites self-defense has become an impractical art of social/economic suicide. Stefan Molyneux

When the fear to offend outweighs the fear to survive you can say to the western world: bye bye

Mass rape of conquering armies of old is what we are witnessing in Germany and Sweden today.

They don't understand those failed states are the way they are because of the people who live there.

No concept of morality outside the west--you take what you can as long as benefits outweigh costs.

Europe is a dusty collection of dead empires and new arrivals are the maggots on it's corpse. Black Pigeon

Who the hell is Merkel to decide what are German values? Certainly not this but she's not budging.

Who is Merkel to decide what are German values? Certainly not this but she won't budge ya know.

Who knew globalism meant communism, open borders, hostile invasion and abolishing culture?

LE FEMME and the Communist Spirit

True: Illegal immigration has decimated black communities but the media never talks about this.

"All cultures are alike" abandons all ideals of architecture, math, beauty--it's sophistry/malarkey.

Sheer depth and richness of texture in arts and sciences meant the west had no equal in the world.

See this: As a couple you're all alone in nature then someone moves in next door--joy no more!

The righteous sees evil that's coming and gets out the way, the evil say "what the heck, it'll be ok".

20 years in desert solitude then moved into country neighborhood and wow, have to build a wall.

Two kinds of elites: lions relying on strength and moral character vs. foxes who win by cunning.

Emigrate, colonize, then "what happened?" when it's too late and we wake up in a foreign country.

The biggest racism today is white-on-white racism. Stefan Molyneux

Guilt cultures stabilize society but always lose with attack cultures who never feel guilty.

They give you the impression whites are attacking blacks to make them look like the victims.

When outcomes of blacks vs. whites don't turn out same we blame whites not genetic differences.

Affirmative action is: gaining advantage at the expense of others.

Mexico accepted money from the U.S. government for that territory so their moral claim is silly.

LE FEMME and the Communist Spirit

They don't come here cuz they love Thomas Jefferson but for the money, called "quality of life".

They're here for cold economic reasons and have no loyalty to the United States.

The problem is black inability not white oppression. Jared Taylor

Yes Asians have a higher IQ but no conformist nation can ever produce a scientific revolution.

The white race is a sinking ship but this can still be turned around--just start speaking, it's legit.

I don't get triggered anymore cuz I don't have people around who trigger me--walls made me free.

Watch who you take in. Stop the hippie commune thing it's wrecking everything. These are spirits, see?

You like nice things so they all want to live with you, see? But third parties are your end--be free.

See Color of Crime. Shootings: blacks 31x and Hispanics 12x more likely than whites to murder.

We will burn Europe to the ground. Tayyip Erdoğan
Migrant violence and terror is "Europe's fault, not linked to mass immigration". Macron

For every black attacked by a white, twelve whites are attacked by blacks and that's a fact.

Whites are the first people in history to be gladly dispossessed of honor, land, country.

Whites are the first people in history to gladly say: "sure, take my land, diminish my power."

Since whites have sub-replacement fertility their only answer is polygamy or extinct by 2050.

LE FEMME and the Communist Spirit

Diversity is not our strength as lost uniqueness means blobs. Race realism is true and we hate mobs.

Whites deferred gratification and restrained fierceness and thus they built the European castles.

Low IQ pops go right on the dole and you think that's good stuff well then you and I are done.

It's not fat but the speed of collecting water. It's released in a moment, removing the fetter.

No society survives once diversity is introduced but we have to: coming unglued/ugly feuds.

With forced diversity instead of loving the strangers with time it leads to hate/see em as slime.

He may be a professor but sounds like a fool.

It's not whites holding blacks back but illegal aliens taking the jobs but they won't face that.

Blacks have a weird affinity to illegals when the latter take away their jobs, housing and hospitals.

By coming here illegally they are all criminals and *because* of that they need to be deported.

A striking reverse association between population density and happiness: wide open spaces = bliss.

Nothing could help blacks more than a wall and deportations. But liberals hate all that, corrupted.

Islam uses demography/migration as tools of asymmetric warfare yet elite dictum is: have no care!

What makes it different is these upsets are scripturally prescribed, approved and mandated.

LE FEMME and the Communist Spirit

Let's be kind to them so they be kind to us when a majority: good luck on that false reality.

If I had to be under a slaveowner let him be white. Jared Taylor

Survival depends on wall (total control) and Muslim Ban (violent ideology vs. founding principals).

Elitism: Islam is nice/tolerant and the west has been nasty to it; land not ours but whoever wants it.

A spectacular double-standard: what is taken for granted by out-groups is denied to whites, pooh.

NO non-white nation would ever let in mass immigration. It's preposterous to think of it even.

Every other group can organize along racial lines--only whites bring reaction, what's going on?

Poisonous anti-white atmosphere of universities: "my group is nothing to be proud of" tragedy.

In this era of crazed anti-racial discrimination they would ban whites due to skin color? Yah sir

Staggering hypocrisy, spectacular injustice as whites diminish into complete disappearance.

Pathological altruism (letting em all in) is a soft form of cultural suicide. Stefan Molyneux

Race realism vs. new age: racial differences 100% environmental otherwise everyone's equal.

Race realism vs. new age: race differences 100% environmental otherwise everyone's equal.

Socialism: philosophy of failure, creed of ignorance, gospel of envy, equal sharing of misery. Churchill

LE FEMME and the Communist Spirit

Born dumb, stay dumb. Born smart, stay smart--minus a few points lost due to trauma.

NEW Italy gets more police/prisons as it clears illegal "gypsy" settlements in towns/cities.

Jerry Brown's "citizens of the economy" means us being cogs in the wheel of global capitalism.

It's common knowledge today but in the 80's they locked up and drugged people thinking like this.

If you said globalist Builderbergers in the 70's it was mandatory drugging for sure but now it's clear.

Every other group can organize along racial lines but not us? Please explain this.

Causes of mass immigration are cleverly concealed by elites but falsely portrayed as inevitable.

Kalergi: Future world citizens a new mixed breed resulting from mass immigration/miscegenation.

Kalergi: Europeans interbreed with non-whites/Asians for a brown pop without identity/easily controlled.
Kalergi: Ethnic separatist movements combined with mass migration = way to destroy the nations.

Kalergi: In order for Europe to be controlled by an elite there must be a homogeneous mixed breed.

Thinking Europeans should fold tradition into one mixed race promotes policies for minority interests.

Merkel won prestigious prize of Kalergi Foundation for excellence promoting this criminal plan.

Multiculturalism: weakened disparate population without national, historical or cultural cohesion.

LE FEMME and the Communist Spirit

Kalergi plan is used by governments intent on genocide of European pops thru mass immigration.

UN: Limit births and promote mixed marriages creating a single world race directed by a central authority.

As Europeans are made the renounce their origins they're to welcome the brown "children of Kalergi"

Kalergi Plan advanced stage: Fusion of Europe with Third World.

The globalists want blind consumers so tell us give up traditions/identity as humanitarians of the world.

European integration amounts to genocide so not telling em is national suicide.

As they prioritize those skipping the line they make legit immigrants wait longer, that's Canada.

For me this diversity crap started at fifteen and overnight life went mean.

When whites won't speak against enemy (fear of being called "racist") they bring out the worst.

Attacking people for things they didn't do by how they look: you're on board with it, I'm not.

Queen hates modernity and I don't blame her cuz it's false theories pursuant to globalist misery.

Multiculturalism is a modern political ideology which is used as a battering ram sanctioning a tragedy.

Opposing the myth, multiculturalism doesn't bring prosperity but poverty and lack of trust/enemies.

We need zero-pop for *them* not us, we need polygamy or we'll go extinct before century is up.

LE FEMME and the Communist Spirit

Only way of fighting back is by excluding Islam from the West hermetically and permanently.

Diversity means: Forcing us to live with people we're not compatible with--it's empty and mean.

Forcing people on us is great cruelty. God's wrath is: being suddenly surrounded by strangers.

God's wrath is: natural disasters or being suddenly surrounded by strangers.

See how cruel diversity is to stop it. Problem is gradually adapting to it then suddenly waking to it.

Inside humans is robotic circuitry of aversion to diversity, a survival device of great value today.

No diversity around red mountains today but I fear Islamic invasion since it's polygamy-friendly.

Gotta think of these things, implications are profound and psychosis-producing to the crowd.

I did my thing: I moved and got a fence and locked gate. Better do it soon or I pity your fate.

Can't stem the tide it's overwhelming glad I'm dying.

Worst torture: people forced on you for a moment or more.

Globalist mindset imposed thru schools always sells it as cool and it's picked up by fools.

It's so bad they're leaving their country to flee it in order to come here and make you submit to it.

Don't go to France if you can't speak Arabic.

Royal wedding not a celebration of British values but multiculturalism, Marxism, black liberation.

LE FEMME and the Communist Spirit

Stop complaining about your guests and blame open borders instead.

7 billion people and most are retarded by design--this explains your trouble keeping friends.

They'll do anything to find racism to justify vastly different outcomes when it's all IQ you bums.

Whites: The reason you are demonized constantly is cuz they want what you have desperately.

It's all OUR fault they are bad. There is no other explanation for it the school authorities said.

Globalists are an anti-human anti-free speech religion and they even call it that in documents.

What a sadistic plan: being demoted by crowds of brutal rapacious strangers is hell man.

First they get rid of other religions then align with Islam cuz it's authoritarian: that's the plan.

Tommy Robinson has been disappeared and they're told to not report it. UK is evil/Theresa Mae

UK put an order out that no one's allowed to talk about it. This is Soviet style tyranny folks.

REVOLUTION: Demonstrators storm the UK government, sick of the torment

The government of the UK is an outside globalist force. Brexit: attempt to get gov back on course.

This is the beginning of the second world revolution against the globalists, Jacobins and parasites.

Humanity will no longer be manipulated by Bezos wanting to bring millions in, weaponized against us.

LE FEMME and the Communist Spirit

Just like when Hitler bombed the Brits thinking they'd roll over. The Brits always turnover.

Brits were 65% against war until Hitler bombed then they were 85% FOR: watch what happens now.

Half of all Americans live in sanctuaries protecting immigrants.

Instead of extreme discernment resulting in merriment you let them all in from a failed experiment.

Ireland has referendum on lowering birthrate but no country can vote on their third world immigrants?

No nation can vote against toxic third world onslaught but they can to kill babies--globalist plot?

You can have feminist-inspired abortion or demographically flourishing population but not both.

Choose: mass immigration or pro-life sentiments. There is no other option even nationalism.

Ireland has just made it's own contribution to Europe's descent into a secular globalist abyss.

Though only 10% pop, Muslims vote as a block so people get into power and we're forsook.

Nationalist populism is fueled by pervasive and deep anti-elite sentiment: we're sick of em.

Any positive representation of white people's history, culture or capabilities is inherently "racist".

Achievements of non-whites are transformed into collective accomplishments of that race.

The media's goal is that whites have no part in mass culture at all.

LE FEMME and the Communist Spirit

Marxists want open borders--they despise Christian culture and know barbarians would crush her.

Now we know why they're here--to be voters--how do we get rid of em faster?

Reasoning: Muslims would never do this so they didn't do this and if they did they're not Muslims.

Systemic racism/unconscious bias: that's all we hear when before it was all ok with them and us.

When everyone does better, civilization/prosperity. But the globalists want us to live under austerity.

Focus on Islam removes the heat from those orchestrating it all but soon it'll be totally outa control.

Italy is giving us hope. New coalition is planning to dump half mil migrants-- they're like Trump.

Migrants in Italy are getting leery as new gov encroaches to either deport them or pull their money.

Save the nation! Far-right Italian parties plot array of sweeping curbs on asylum/immigration.

They're gonna get em: Landlord confrontation/new centers of detention ready for deportation.

Imams registered with state, unauthorized mosques closed and no new ones- -shut that gate.

People are waking/rising up against the managed decline of Europe and those letting her fall.

And to think it's the churches investing in open borders--like the Lutheran council making a bundle.

It hurts feeling a stranger in a strange land but when it's your home it's a real disaster happening.

LE FEMME and the Communist Spirit

They're coming in like a flood. Stop the churches Trump cuz they're the investors making a lump.

So the churches are traitors flooding us with strangers? That's amazing when you think about it.

What if deacon came to your home and opened the door to thugs? There is no difference--need Trump

Churches think they're being Christian by flooding us with strangers. Virtue signaling = dangerous.

In the UK they say "run, hide, tell" to the ancestors of World War II, what hell.

I was invaded by thugs of both genders over several decades and I say open borders is Hades.

They destroy all that is precious to you. It's no different than an rapacious army marching through.

Animals are tearing up the beautiful European countrysides, the little villages history describes.

Everything you hold dear they think nothing of destroying cuz it's a totally different tribe I fear.

Lutheran Council is one traitor selling us out for cash. Each migrant brings a price once processed.

There is no end to appeasement.

They are completely different from us--opposed diametrically, genetically and culturally

Despicable traitors brought in an invading army for votes and money.

Millions of hostile invaders flooding into the land.

You must throw off the guilt the elites have been programming and tormenting you with.

LE FEMME and the Communist Spirit

By letting in low IQ pops--the dumb--they'll go along with anything, nation of controlled bums.

Germans the smartest scientists and musicians or revert to the total opposite, Merkel's non-logic

Genocide need not be a mass slaughter but just telling em not to breed while nourishing others.

White genocide: encouraging abortion then bring in those with 20 children and support all of em.

Long term plan: Replace uppity whites by telling em to abort then bring in high-fertility alien pops.

It is so evil, well-thought out, disgusting, criminal, unheard of, beyond shocking: 100 year planning.

Genocide isn't always violent, just Impose measures intended to limit births within a group.

Genocide doesn't have to be concentration camps, rounding people up, or execution. Just a decision.

Genocide: flood country with invaders hostile to indigenous peoples or founders of that nation.
Take over government then let in a swamping wave of foreigners to aggressively colonize that nation.

A hostile group uses the state power to ensure migrants get benefits, housing, medical and cash.

Government gives em the benefits to breed rapidly once settled in our homeland/fat and happy.

Mass immigration is not accidental but by design.

In the hearts of Europe's peoples is an ancient fear of loss of homeland to Islamic invaders.

LE FEMME and the Communist Spirit

YAY: Soro's audacious attempt to install a pro-EU technocrat as Italy's Prime Minister has failed.

There's a big difference between being welcoming and giving strangers the keys to your house.

They pretend to be conservatives or even nationalists but suddenly you see they sure aren't it.

Whatever the people want they get the opposite and what politicians want the people reject.

Elites live in gated communities with armed guards so don't mind the floods of strangers in mobs.

They lie to the people, spend all time virtue signaling and have pure contempt for the native pop.

Dear Scots: Your leaders don't care about you--they're just importing votes/signaling virtue.

The implications of their policies or the fact they'd even consider them is enough: ban em.

E-Race White: That's why the globalists push abortion--white genocide.

Anti-bullying means anti-Islamaphobia.
Libs see nationalism as silly tribalism we shoulda outgrown by now.

Now flying our flag means we are intolerant of immigrants or just flat-out racist.

Socialism is poison and a poisonous idea is destruction.

The decline of the west is so into the latter stages we no longer have the will to fight savages.

To destroy/displace a culture you need psychology, mainstream media and institutional support.

LE FEMME and the Communist Spirit

Elites want a despondent pathology displacing the nationalistic and optimistic Europeans.

The special quality of group's defended territory is insulation from demographic disturbance.

A group can suffer setbacks but as long as it has it's territorial space it can recover.

Territory ensures survival. Mass immigration diminishes genetic interests of the native pops.

Multicultural surrender = pathological, pro-white against displacement = adaptive/rational.

The more I have land (my territory) and a fence then demographic changes effect me less.

A free society requires high IQ populations, and there is not one low IQ pop on earth that is free.

Immigration is a government program and immigrants are here for the subsidies in general.

Building first world economies pulls up the third world, lowering first world to be equal does not.

We don't want em here!
Is there any doubt in Planet X or do we now have two suns? The gravitic effects are the earth's hex.

Globalism is coming to an end in Europe along with the whole notion of multiculturalism.

With globalization the host nation must accommodate the immigrants: the backlash is now, thanks!

It's a strange era when bad reputation marks good character, victimized by the worst on earth.

LE FEMME and the Communist Spirit

A secular globalist world can only exist by attacking the religious values of our traditions/past.

Emancipatory politics: power of the state used to disentrench us from our traditions/roots.

Globalism sees traditional roots as constraints to our true selves or is that just what they say?

Justice, equality and liberty in a globalized society: What a total mess that turned out to be.

Give me your tired, your poor and those who want a free WIFI connection. Michelle Malkin

Although IQ is stable one can still degrade through sin, association or being disabled.

Biggest reason for population replacement immigration: white guilt, western ethnomasochism.

Replacism: Interchangeability, the false idea you can replace anything and it will be the same.

Replacism: False idea of the insignificance and irrelevance of the thing being replaced, like us.

High taxes de-incentivizes Europeans from births and incentivizes immigrants to come to the west.
Trump will put a tariff on Canadian cars and they'll make em here. He's so smart, a genius/seer.

How hegemonies keep their empire: keep everyone off balance adversaries and allies alike.

Champagne socialists push diversity to please the youth while not having to live with the poop.

Throwing acid in one's face with goal of disfigurement is a foreign and barbaric practice.

LE FEMME and the Communist Spirit

As London becomes less British it has a higher crime rate/more badness.

Einstein was a xenophobe just like me. He hated strange, brutish foreign customs and freaks.

Democrats ruin every city they run cuz they're globalists: debauched and evil not homespun.

Merkel is facing mutiny over her mad, dangerous open door migration policy.

Merkel madness is about to topple and I'm so glad she's been murderously awful for her people.

How does evil Soros get his political gain? My overseeing Europe's "managed decline".

Throwing Tommy Robinson into prison population is like throwing a baby to the shark's ocean.

Military is trained for zombie patrol cuz they know huge hordes of people will be outa control.

UN has said global pandemic is the only savior of world government seen as the solution.

Our country's not for everyone, you must give back to it.

If whites don't start having *many* babies America will be a third world s--t hole country.
You can have open borders or welfare state but not both cuz they come for free stuff/it's destroyed.

"Detained children" ginned up by globalists for open borders, cheap labor and democrat voters.

Whole gist: If you don't wanna be separated from your family don't cross the border illegally.

We've gotta have borders and there's consequences if you cross illegally/become a criminal now.

LE FEMME and the Communist Spirit

If you don't know your history you get to repeat it until you learn it or you die.

They're displacing Europeans with docile, dependent welfare slaves who won't challenge authority.

They don't want integration, it's all about bringing people in who don't want small gov/liberty at all.

Only 3% get jobs, they were brought in as dependent slobs with the goal of socialist control.

Paradise is small government and liberty but these aliens wanna be paid for by you and me.

We used to happily walk to concerts but now worry about knives in a totally different mindset.

There's big money/LOOT in all aspects of climate change and that has corrupted science.

Exporting billions to countries who don't play fair then buy up America. Trump says: no more!

Merkel is a total failure and everyone knows it: "We're sick of you witch, good riddance!"

Don't you wanna control your own destiny? Why prefer some unelected bureaucrat's tyranny?

If they don't know about private property it's scary cuz they'll take your stuff if given the upper hand.

We all want the EU gone but if their policing of the internet is achieved, we lose and they've won.

In the tyrannical EU today, democracy and opinion is only permitted when you vote the right way.

Those who care more for members of other countries than their own don't love anyone.

LE FEMME and the Communist Spirit

You have no idea how evil the socialist communist Obama is. He demeaned America/all of us.

Liberals want no borders/for America to be crowded with foreign people and they're not evil?

It's gotta be a full-on patriot not some RINO playing the same games as Clinton. Dig deep, amen.

If you're not protecting borders you're also not protecting the inside of the nation, it's values.

Democrats manufactured border hysteria for votes.

Islam the sexist religion of the world, with women 1/2 a man but liberals love it (even the girls).

Race hustlers are cowards on a foundation of lies, Satan's sand. Confront with truth/they run.

Race hustlers speak so fast/smooth you don't know they're lying but they are, making millions.

According to rules you don't go on dole unless here legally for five years yet leeches everywhere.

In Italy the left has imploded totally and thus marks the direction of other European countries.

The more the left insults us the more the right rewards us. Matteo Salvini

"World Citizen" is the notion pushed by neoMarxists and the UN.: it's all about open borders man.

Nations and cultures no longer matter in a matrix of World Citizenship but we still gotta pay for it.

Go to any elementary school--they see themselves as world citizens not Americans my friends.

LE FEMME and the Communist Spirit

Entering a new world of the right--nationalism, populism, traditionalism--and what light!

Russian youth are the most pro-Putin, patriotic, nationalistic and religious of any generation, gosh.

Boring, hideous and cruel: becoming a standardized multicultural liberal globalist enterprise.

Sleeper cell traitor Obama, enemy of America

Liberals demand aliens' court hearing but our dear leader says NO--send em back now not later.

The RINO republicans are as bad as democrats, supporting their donors for the open borders.

They want borders in their lives yet not in yours but hypocrisy no more cuz we're in Trump's world.

Enormous amount of black on white violence all across the country and all unreported by the press.

Critical Racism taught in the schools: racism is everywhere and permanent they say to new fools.

The corporate media hypes racial division 24/7 and the culprit's always the white men.

Liberal news is eliminating comment sections cuz it's all conservative complaints against em.

Fired for telling the TRUTH about black-on-white racial violence.

"Around blacks never relax". Employee fired for these words: facts.

Foreign nationals flooding the border are called unaccompanied children as a deceiver.

It's a corporate funded Maoist uprising.

LE FEMME and the Communist Spirit

Black on elder (old people) violence: When it comes to "racism" they still refuse to believe it.

Black on Asian violence is so bad it's called Frisco's "dirty little secret" about poor storeowners.

"But whites are doing this too" NOT TRUE.

Lies we bought: Obama introduced concept that all disparity in outcome was white people's fault.

Critical Race Theory: Blacks are relentless victims of relentless white racism--one reality.

Critical race theory (whites are demons) is taught to children let alone colleges where it's Religion.

The greatest lie of this generation is black people are relentless victims of whites the culprits.

Subconscious Racism: We are guilty for something we're not even aware of--that's the plan.

Whites are like evil tigers who are just gonna maul blacks everywhere: that's the myth declared.

What is a racist? A conservative winning an argument with a liberal. Peter Brimelow

Democrats were the KKK and against equality.

Affirmative Action quotas enormous: the unfairness is damaging while the basis is erroneous.

UK universities tinker with white scores, severely reduce Asian and pump up black, no kiddin'

Affirmative Action theory: you're so bad we've gotta force people to hire you/put you first too.

LE FEMME and the Communist Spirit

A black gets into Princeton/must choose: physics/math or Afro resentment in Black schools.

Stop using a hyphen and be an American.

White racism unmentioned by never-Trumpers.

Children of the Lie want to bring in non-whites who are socialists from s--thole countries.

The immigrants coming in are brainwashed to hate white people seduced by free stuff/meals.

Children of the Lie seek to reduce white culture by migrants used to tyranny/socialist lures.

They want a black takeover of America and this idea makes us shudder cuz we'll be done, over.

Just look at the violence, lack of respect, nastiness and ghetto dirtiness of the black cities.

Europe is gone, it's over, a ghetto. Don't let it happen to America the greatest country known.

In Europe whites don't have freedom to disagree with the POCs (people of color). Amazing?

"F--k borders, F--K walls" as left is desperate to start civil war around ICE headquarters.
Merkel is finished, it's just a matter of when. She's ruined Germany so can now enjoy retirement.

The more they go down the Bernie Sanders socialist path the more they'll lose elections/relevance.

The youth want full on socialism but no thank you I want to keep my money not give it to bums.

Socialism is inherently authoritarian since you confiscate from me then redistribute for free.

LE FEMME and the Communist Spirit

Redistribute until wealthy are bled dry and the impoverished majority becomes a dead country.

Socialism has killed 100 million people in the last century. How can the left want this misery?

Harsh punishments like amputation vs. mercy, forgiveness and salvation then God forgets it son.

What kind of merciful God would chop off something so beautiful as a hand for stealing an egg?

The left are sick freaks--we know that--but violently want open borders to totally wreck us.

Psychologists have become democrat confessors instilling the filthy globalist liberal agenda.

They're at war with prosperity/capitalism, foolish tools of the globalist agenda to take us down.

Their viewpoint is media-induced and group-controlled--they won't give it up till sick and old.

Collapse third world, put socialist/communists in charge, remove western borders = fascist world.

When college professors light the fuse the most violent revolutions come through students.

Beating people over the head with clubs and if you fight back they call it a riot.

Everywhere a socialist gets in they become communist and it's always a nightmare scenario, honest.

Globalists concocted this whole operation of mass immigration pursuing a classless system.

Communism creates mass starvation.

LE FEMME and the Communist Spirit

It is your job to invade El Norte and take up residence in the United States. Mexico President Obrador

The Plan: People fleeing failing communism then destroy their new countries they reside in.

Flee collapsing communism in more than half of the nations then destroy whoever takes em in.

Like dominoes falling: they're fleeing collapsing nations only to destabilize new ones (like Chile).

You establish crisis centers where they're at not add military age men when only 10% get jobs.

Dominoes: Collapse Latin America into Mexico/Us, collapse Africa and Middle East into Europe.

Making their move to world government by collapsing third world pops into giant migrant waves.

Radical Islam allied with Soros-funded left and international combine.

Millennials overwhelmingly prefer socialism cuz they don't know what it is: disaster/utopian vision.

Do what the people want/voted you in for and you'll SURGE in the polls--obvious but not to fools.

We have to stop seeing ourselves as the underdog cuz we're not--we have the *peoples* on our side.
You feel vulnerable and powerless with floods of foreigners invading while you can do nothing.

Wicked men wanna get in your home cuz there you're in control and they want your gold.

Mexicans call black people names. They look down on em, the myth they get along is just fake.

There is no multicultural unity, they hate each other.

LE FEMME and the Communist Spirit

They push a false idea we all get along and it's NOT TRUE!

We invited them into our home and they turned, giving us the finger. Make em go back/no linger.

Our differences don't make us stronger it's our similarities bringing us together to storm the weather.

Affirmative action is at a crossroads. Trump said we'll no more use race as a diversity code.

The dirty dems wanna bring millions more in and they can do any awful thing they'll be forgiven.

Evil is dissolving every minute. It's a snowball effect as Trump was in it. A bad memory, forget it.

Trump offers Pocahontas ONE MIL to prove Indian heritage as audacity destroys arrogance

Socialism always ends in poverty and violence but you think this time it won't/why take a chance?

What would you do if a million foreigners walked thru your land and pooped everywhere, man?

Not just "demographic change" but moving from happy light to depressed dark/not about skin color.

What would you do if a foreign mob trudged thru your front yard and killed your cats and dogs?

We gotta keep em out--they're not refugees but economic migrants, just want the money honey.

One damnable heresy is forgiveness without repentance, making em into recidivist criminals.

If you want open borders you hate blacks, cuz illegal immigrants are taking their jobs and tax.

LE FEMME and the Communist Spirit

Those who are part of this world are Prophets of Baal.

There's a plan in place and it's all gonna happen so prepare for panic and great civil unrest even.

The royal wedding not a celebration of England but multiculturalism and cultural Marxism.

Whites celebrating diversity are rejoicing at their declining numbers and influence, a monstrosity.

Getting the right people in power like Salvini/Kurtz will invoke the true history of Islamic invasion.

Immigration--who's behind it? The same people trying to cover it up. START

Anyone with a US flag is my friend. We're drawing closer since this last decade of being scammed.

A cuckholded country lets strangers in it's house and it's a disgusting thing done by lush/louse.

Trump showed Theresa Mae how to do Brexit but she wrecked it so the deal's off you twit.

Nationalist populism is here to stay so you just better get used to it. Dr. Steve Turley

Paradox: The less diverse the area the more they're all for diversity, enigma. Keligeri Plan: Flood white countries with POCs (people of color) to change demography forever.

Third world cultures don't think the way we do nor have the same IQ and we'll see the results soon.

One result of multiculturalism is unsecured borders since that would be mean to the invaders.

High immigration = loss of culture.

LE FEMME and the Communist Spirit

New level new devil need a higher wall because tho' they know nothing they can still be cruel.

Just because they're dumb doesn't mean harmless, they're dangerous because they're dumb.

It's all about immigration, immigration, immigration. Ann Coulter

These people can do no wrong while the good guy's put away. Innocent men jailed for being white, ok?

RINO republicans pretend they'll do the right thing but once in become democrats stealin' and lyin'.

If you embrace the collapse I hope you bought gold and silver. Metals: the only hedge of the clever.

Listen: Since a man's job is to protect his family he'd never be for open borders by definition.

Putin-Trump dyad is wonderful cuz he's a Christian and vicious invaders, he won't let em in.

Putin is a fox, he's so clever. Listen carefully cuz whatever he says, he's saying something else.

Always a sub-text to what the man Putin is saying. Complicated, wow factor, clever, daring.

Savor Putin like a famous chess match.
Ha ha "Yah I know about dossiers" said Putin, the ex-KGB who faked em to discredit disagreers.

Christian vs. Muslim extremists and radicals: How can you compare a tiny few to the many thousands?

"We used to create dossiers" meaning he can send him to a gulog. Ha ha He's as great as Trump.

Putin sees that it's not our laws but secret backdoor behind the scenes agreements with cops.

LE FEMME and the Communist Spirit

"In a democracy it should be a court" (Putin) not saying USA has become totalitarian of course.

The center left is sliding in with Marxian fanatics that can't be reasoned with so give up and live.

Exclusionary attitudes increase with demographic change not decrease to accept the strange.

Their stance is: no borders, it's a human right for everyone in the world to immigrate to the US.

Diverse societies are much harder to govern than homogeneous ones, that's obvious hon'

Encroaching diversity quickly changes champagne suburban socialists into republican exclusionists.

Groups are all different, like how they handle the trash--the little things bring the greatest clash.

Increaasingly people of color are changing identity to "white" so census may show a white majority yet.

Racially motivated weaponized altruism has failed.

South Africa was empty/dry then whites created paradise and blacks said "you stole it, it's mine".

It only goes one way. When whites are majority they give blacks breaks but never the opposite, ok?

"Everyone's the same so bad outcomes due to prejudice/injustice"--false, it's IQ differences.

They're not the same. There are tall races, short races, smart races and dumb races (lame).

Myth of the century: All differences in group outcome are the results of prejudice and bigotry.

248

LE FEMME and the Communist Spirit

Why are blacks poor in Africa? "Cuz the whites stole everything/raped our women" false again.

Radical anti-scientific humanist egalitarianism says: All humans are the same and our friends.

Watch out for this or we're dead Americans: "Everyone's the same, all differences due to racism"

Communists weaponizing visible minorities started in 1920's and we see the horrible results today.

It's no ones fault that groups have different levels of intelligence but to deny it is incredulous.

Rather than admit to varying IQ they will drive out/kill the farmers supporting the country too.

So much anger they drive out the greatest workers keeping the country alive/out of danger.

Average South African farmer feeds 2000 people so take out 15,000 farmers = 30 million/no food.

South African farming is very complicated and average IQ of blacks is <74 and they can't work it.

They see socialism as a magic bullet when all it does is wreck society and then fully destroy it.
Pathological white guilt: We're so sorry we gave the world science, medicine and freedom still!

Whites gave the world medicine so now we're as bad as Genghis Khan? START

Fifty whites murdered each day in South Africa, that's one every 20 minutes/still they lie to ya.

RINOS who hate Trump invaded Iraq for no reason/wouldn't admit the mistake/killed Kadafi as fake.

LE FEMME and the Communist Spirit

Hillary's server was a drop box to foreign countries to sell all our secrets to friends or enemies.

America and the free market is sexy and communism sux. Jones, Alex

Africa was dry wasteland until whites made it paradise again then blacks said "you stole it friend".

Ethiopians 63 IQ, Americans 100 IQ and you call that equal you fools?

Wearing a MAGA hat is now dangerous so travel in strong man groups, it's most advantageous.

Us surrender/subsume OUR culture to a worldwide system? You gotta be kiddin'

We're losing our country: when good men stand up they're called racist but we can't back down.

As floods of the third world come in they are taught to hate white people and Trump sees evil.

This country is worth fighting for so close the back door and the rest deport.

White people must start having babies. Do what the Mormons do: have em 'til God says stop.

We're well on our way to being a third world ghetto country. That's what president said: urgency.

When they come from s-hole countries they bring that environment. Look around you, it's not us.

The invaders have a socialist mentality so they drain the government, are schooled how to do it.

Globalist media gives false impressions that blacks and Hispanics get along like cousins.

Blacks are fighting back being imposed upon, but in Mexico considered second class citizens.

LE FEMME and the Communist Spirit

Invaders hate blacks and run em outa their own communities yet blacks still vote for like treacheries.

They're total groupies. If one wins they all win, if you criticize one they all feel shunned.

You're black and vote democrat for a dirty rat who lets strangers in to make you sad sacks?

Hispanic tribalism: You hit one and they all come after you, always outnumbering the poor few.

Due to Hispanic invasion black people are dying/being forced outa Los Angeles--care about this?

Globalist media won't report Hispanic-Black violence cuz it goes against the multicultural matrix.

First white flight outa cities now black flight cuz they're scared of the Mexicans, there I said it.

Killing an unknown person is an initiation right and most times he's black in a nightmare fight.

Try to find a black politician and he'll talk thru you or walk off--you can never corner em.

Los Angeles is not diversity it's Mexico.

Ultimate Darwinism: Both liberals and minorities center in cities destroyed by what's coming.

Country folk are better prepared/won't suffer the mass violence and Mad Max of the cities.

Afraid of getting involved with Mexicans cuz if one's mad you're targeted by all their cousins.

Even NBC sees socialists are after your money, will fight you for the crumbs on your table honey

LE FEMME and the Communist Spirit

They want you to think whites are the problem and that blacks/Latinos get along: WRONG.

Blacks are being murdered by Mexican gangs and one initiation rite is to kill an unknown.

Dems: Wherever they want power they bring in the people of color.

White Americans easily used due to their false compassion but in other countries there is none.

It's not about gender/color but what's right or wrong and you have whole groups for the latter.

Knockout games, robbing/rapes: there's a race war going on but it's one-sided against whites.

Race war against whites is being supported by liberal media, democrats and RINO republicans.

They wanna outnumber white Americans.

In L.A. there's a major war between resident blacks and Mexicans esp the new ones flooding in.

There's third world racist prejudice and they're killing resident blacks in L.A.'s ghetto streets.

Why do they segregate blacks from Mexicans in prisons? Cuza what's happening in L.A. now son.

The democrats have fully embraced Bernie Sanders socialism and Maxine Waters nuttiness.

Zimbabwe went from the breadbasket of Africa to the basket case and now it's happening twice.

There are no successful black nations on earth. Foreign Policy Magazine

LE FEMME and the Communist Spirit

What does the caravan of low IQs do to host nations? It is horrifying since IQ determines kindness.

IQ pops of 98 and above all have highly developed nation states. The others, forget it mate.

IQ of 85 and below show poverty and social/institutional dysfunction, thought you should know.

An average IQ of 97 is necessary for a nation's success. Black Pidgeon

Latin American invaders have an average IQ of 81--wow what fun, our democracy will be gone.

Low IQ invaders wouldn't even be eligible for military service in the US and you say we need this?

High IQ nations are breaking as low IQ pops are busting thru Europe cuz they're much crueler.

Europe sees its stable, democratic, low crime, low corruption and wealthy modern society crumble.

Italians are extremely unhappy about the integrationist positions the EU wants them taking.

Race differences in IQ explains everything that's happening but we can't talk about it unfortunately.

Americans don't care about Russia so shut up about it.
Ethnic underbelly of kids not raised well knowing nothing but rioting, violence and vandalism.

You can't hate blacks but it's perfectly ok (politically correct) to hate whites.

Let's be kind to them so they be kind to us when a majority: good luck on that false reality.

Deep State fears peace between U.S. and Russia, that explains a lot.

You can't explain how they're wrong cuz low IQ limits the dumb throng.

LE FEMME and the Communist Spirit

Britain is losing it's culture due to immigration and it'll never be same if you don't act soon. Trump

Whenever you feel bleak/persecuted think of Tommy or Dinesh rotting in jail/putting up with it.

All censorship is geared towards the nationalist populist right and none of it at the leftist blight.

The Alex Jones ban will fuel populism all over the world, just like when Tommy Robinson got burned.

Liberal politically correct sites are celebrated/right is banned but watch for the Streisand Effect.

Drudge, the most trafficked site in the world gives links to Alex Jones updates: Greatness.

The Alex Jones Ban will fuel us more than ever, it's just what we needed and our good end is near.

We'll talk about Alex Jones Ban so much they will see they CAN'T silence neither AJ or us man.

Cortez: Let's see, what do they want to hear? What kinda person should I be to be most popular?

Politically correct suffer from excess of impulsive compassion for those on bottom/hate the rich.
Trump Derangement Syndrome is interesting/deep but ramifications are scary with these creeps.

The growing hatred for whites was subliminal but with Trump it mushroomed and we see it now.

Not only is he the hated white he's rich too/even worse he gets the girls and it's just too much sir.

Due to Trump people can finally say what they want to say, not like that commie Obama we hate.

LE FEMME and the Communist Spirit

Politicians encourage in-group preference to vote as one but not when it comes to whites/they're done.

Trump gave whites the most powerful thing of all: in-group preference and will to defend themselves.

Donald Trump encouraged white people to act as a group with their own interests at heart/new.

Anti-white policies of corporate world: affirmative action, thought crimes, liberal youth CEOs.

From charming towns where we all know em to segregated slums where no one speaks/no fun.

Why have confidence in the captain of your ship if she steers in to an iceberg? Socialism has 100% rate of failure.

You don't need a loopy old crank forcing you to walk off the plank.

Replacism: False idea of the insignificance and irrelevance of the thing being replaced, like us.

High taxes de-incentivizes Europeans from births and incentivizes immigrants coming to the west.

Trudeau made ass of himself in India so tried to regain in polls by taking on strong man of America.

Wonderful church but it's made up of people. That's where trouble starts--bible says we're all evil.

Christian vs. Muslim extremists and radicals: How can you compare a tiny few to the many thousands?

UK has become an evil land where pedophiles walk free but those reporting on them are in prison.

As London becomes less British it has a higher crime rate/more badness.

LE FEMME and the Communist Spirit

Justin Trudeau's a globalist puppet taking mother and father outa all docs and you like this idiot?

Art of the Deal in North Korea: You're either gonna die in poverty or be rich with great prosperity.

Ocasio-Cortez is not making a good first impression and that is the lasting one.

Ms. Cortez is proudly ignorant and an arrogant liar (grew up in rich suburb not in the Bronx).

Cortez is the poster for opining on issues while knowing nothing about em or making things up.

What scares me: the socialist dumb becoming the majority and no way of explaining to them.

What is big government? A knock at your door. It's clerkism, hierarchies or little creeps with power.

Tyranny doesn't come from distant government but its tentacles which are everywhere you are.

Socialism: the statue of the bureaucrat, man with briefcase--that's where you feel it the most.

One meeting with the briefcase and you're a nutcase cuz you've lost your free will/gov framed.

Papers, papers, papers, you can't do it--knock at the door always looking over shoulder/horror.

Hey--what happened to ISIS? They're gone cuz Trump just told generals to "take care of this"

They complain of white supremacy but all I see is "brown power" signs of La Raza in California.

Cortez: "Abolish profit, prisons, cash bail, borders"--with thousands of murders a year, sure!

LE FEMME and the Communist Spirit

Anti-bullying programs keep Muslims kids from assimilating while making American kids accepting.

They travel in groups, we don't—so when the Swedish lady invites him over a gang rape follows.

They travel in groups with a thousand cousins so don't flub up or knock at your door, threatenin'

Unless we get our backs up it's the end of the white race. They're multiplyin'/we're cowering, afraid.

Rapes on young boys is a sudden new phenomenon due to all the immigration from Afghanistan.

We don't just hate foreign practices now we also hate liberalism and what it's done to children.

I just feel like we're all gonna be eaten up by a bottomless pit brown cavern, strange and brutish.

Those to the south are just as mean/heartless. Must face it: we were the best/flooded with less.

The Nordish far right has burgeoned and now they're competin' to who can be more isolatin'

New nationalist views on border security, immigration quotas, welfare social benefit recipients.
Have hope—when attitudes change re: immigration, policies like welfare also change/they're gone.

Mass immigration means one thing: our piece of the pie will be much smaller/banished altogether.

What's staring us in the face is mass illegal immigration and them flooding your hometown.

Undifferentiated empathy is bad not good. You have to think not just feel, thus creating hoods.

LE FEMME and the Communist Spirit

Sadiq Khan didn't wreck London he was elected because it was already wrecked. Mark Collett

Marginalized by people brought in to replace us. It's a criminal armed invasion and our death.

Rather than establishing own nation they're more comfortable living with us making us feel guilty.

We're a distinct people and not everyone can fit in with ya, what a radical view today in America.

Whether they like it or not, must adapt to the new emerging world order with Trump at the corner.

A RICH time to invest--and not just in metals like silver and gold. Full throttle w/Trump thru God.

Of course we hate that Merkel vermin. She let so many in outa false compassion, that's women.

Feminist illogic: Merkel declares multiculturalism a failure then promptly opens all the borders.

Liberalism: Stop having babies to save resources but then import half the third world to make up for it.

Democrat is no longer the party of the working man but of free stuff. They want socialism and hate Trump.

Autophagy

Divine luster, lustrous, illustrious.

Gluttony a major sin. Bottomless Pit Syndrome unmentioned at church with obesity all around.

LE FEMME and the Communist Spirit

In the autophagiast fasting state the body will suddenly deflate--all cells freed/you're lookin' great.

Divine luster, lustrous, illustrious.

Autophagy heals it all as blood circulates thru each cell and makes it well in a miracle God did tell.

Beauty like health involves a harmonious proportion between parts of the body in relation to the whole.

Tho' eating ludicrous crap, by eating once daily/fasting 20 hours I cured and healed just like that.

If low carb I crave fruit, if high carb I crave fats so to hell with that just eat to your fill then fast.

Being overweight is a health problem that you can change and it's easy with intermittent fast (IF).

8 hour food window now fast 16/GO.

One meal a day fasting is legitimate so refusing to discuss it since it's not longer is ridiculous.

It's ok to eat all you want in one meal then stop--that's all you need for the whole day: Godspeed.

The greatest healer is fasting so eat all you want then joy everlasting.

Eat butter become lustrous

You'll learn to love OMAD (one meal a day) for a skinny/fit bod, charisma and mental clarity.

Stop dieting and rely on autophagy. When you don't eat it dissolves suddenly: it self-digests your fat baby.

What it takes for agelessness/good looks: faith in autophagy is all it took.

LE FEMME and the Communist Spirit

So many undigested meals piling up in the tissues but daily fasting autophagy clears it all out.

Picture the Drano ad--it won't go through twice. Autophagy will save you, just eat big once.

I'm a big flake, a chip off the old block. Flake, flake, flake, then thru autophagy the real Karen Kellock

Get skinny to thrive in your nineties. Become svelte (jettison weight) to be alive with creativities.

Stay fat, drop dead > 60. Get skinny thrive at 90 and be your best (the top of your game) honey.

What keeps me healthy/slim is daily fasting not counting.

The most beautiful model in the world said "at parties I head right for the pies and cakes". Explain.

All dieting is unhealthy constraint, just eat what you want then fast all day.

A healthy body will want to move and eat good food. As health increases so too good moods.

How to get healthy: skip lunch and dinner and do it everyday to get sharper, friskier and skinnier.

Autophagy is when you don't eat the body eats itself, the bad stuff.
Bigger the pieces of skin chippin' off the ol' block the more autophagy is taking place/it rocks.

Autophagy is like a snake getting a new skin.

I build saddlebags thru starch and fats but thru autophagy it all goes down thru the fasting day.

Autophagy--self digestion of bad/fat cells--is only evoked through fasting: eating not one morsel.

LE FEMME and the Communist Spirit

How are they killing us do you suppose? By what goes in our body (food) and on it (our clothes).

It's called "leaven" when they dilute value by adding crap and charging the same and God hates it.

Increasingly they are poisoning us with food and fabrics so store up on whatever works.

Debris pockets around mouth area reflect what you're eating. Fast: it's all gone, brushed out, fleeting.

To eat follow the Satiety Index not the Nutrient Index (surprisingly/who knew) to feel best.

To be happy and energetic eat the most calorically dense for the long haul and this fasting is paleo.

Highest on the satiety index is fat combined with starch. Butter on your spuds, garlic bread gorge.

Eating sparsely (rabbit food) you gotta eat all day and that's not high enough for me, no way.

And then to eat dinner too? That's crazy and the major reason for obesity--do breakfast only.

Always down in the gut digesting. That's a waste of energy--do it once a day and be lookin' good/flyin'.

As a rabbit/monkey food eater I was obsessed with food--it's all I thought about, mentally unglued.

Starch and Friendly Dairy. Alfredo pasta with cheese, garlic bread saturated with butter, oh my!

If you wanna spend your life eating bananas all day go ahead but us cowboys will eat right instead.

Lunch with little, sup with less, better yet go to bed supperless. Benjamin Franklin

LE FEMME and the Communist Spirit

Eat most calorically dense once a day not sparse rabbit food thrice or more but still always hungry.

Candida: Yes there's a bloom after eating but thru the day it goes away as you're fully deflating.

Don't be bitter cuz you're fatter, the women of the fifties ate butter and looked so much better.

Vegetarian dogs get cheese, butter, cream and raw milk: they are ageless, strong and fit.

You don't have to eat three times a day--that's ridiculous. Eat just once and be creative/gracious.

ONE four-hour food window then swing into your fun fabulous fast then be famous today.

Take joy when bloated, tired, fat, lopsided, flaky cuz this is your day to FAST/deflate quickly.

Fasting days are party days as I wait for the benefits accruing speedily thanks to God Almighty.

How to gain most: make yourself least, fast.

You're bloated like a walking water bed. Fast and soon it all flows out and you're joyous instead.

Take joy, today is the fast! You woke up feeling crazy, ugly and bloated--time to have a blast.

Fast and be a child. Leave the left brain behind, don't track your mind, open to God the True Find.

Fast then watch it all drain out. By the mere decision alone these healing forces are set off.

To deny an impulse in respect to a principal: that's how the rewarded fast works, it's so simple.

LE FEMME and the Communist Spirit

Globalists have shrewdly made us ugly thru GMOs but the invaders look good, more in the know.

Ladies cut a salad for him every single day cuz even if he messes up the greens form a defense, ok?

The weight tends to bunch up after thirty unless you do something like eat once a day only.

Each day I seek sun to heal emotions.

At any party I go right for the pies and cakes--that's sugar for energy and fat for satiety.

He looked beautiful and quick at eighty living on morning pastries: sugar for energy/fat for satiety.

Vegetarianism includes dairy which brings satiety meaning long fasting periods equals = healing.

Delicious vegetarianism has always included eggs, fish and dairy vs. veganism: eating all day.

Morning smoothie: high nutrition, low mass.

Best Food Routine: Morning smoothie, Brunch with family, Afternoon Fast, Just Skip Dinner last.

Smoothies for breakfast, salad for lunch then they fend for themselves.
One digestive burn a day: perfect, incredible, energizing. Two: not happening, blocked up, choking.

Let's face it, by being skinny you're more like a racehorse or greyhound, high on thoroughbred scale.

Who wants meso chunky active or endo fatty social? I prefer ecto cerebro (solitude, happily alone).

Ecto cerebro: Eat then don't eat. Lovely luxurious tasty meal then wonderful fast for days untill.

LE FEMME and the Communist Spirit

I don't restrict food groups any more. I eat then don't eat, whatever it is my happy heart adores.

The most beautiful model in the world said "I go right for the pies and cakes"

The richest, fattiest, sweetest, most decadent dessert means greatest satiety longest afterward.

Orthorexia becomes psychosis over food groups and stats and I've had enough of ALL of that.

Life is way too short to be worrying about all this: orthorexia is the pits and most is not legit.

So you ate something wrong, the body has capacity to self-correct so give yourself a break!

What I do restrict is when I eat--my food window. No food later or things don't work, ya know.

Elasticity: inflate (bloat) or deflate (let it go) suddenly. This is the endlessly mutable body.

How did ladies of the fifties have 15" waists so nifty? They weren't afraid of fat/ate it heartily.

Have you seen your synthetic food? That's one reason everyone's a zombie: deluded, crude.

The richer/fattier the food the more healing since satiety power enables longer fasting hours.

I feel good today--its up and down depending on the environment and what i'm doing/eating.

Just fill the stomach so you won't be hungry and just to make sure you eat it make it tasty.

It's what's on your body that gets in it like food/drink is poisonous and they're trying to kill us.

LE FEMME and the Communist Spirit

It's what's on your body that gets in it. Clothes are made poisonous cuz they're trying to kill us.

Fabric companies are adulterating everything, it's called "lacing" and it's just as poisonous, hey.

Noodles are the way to do it. It's already done and fills the tum.

It's not just that Macdonalds makes you fat and sick but that China is a collapsing hell hole, heck.

Don't eat food outa China, the collapsing hell hole--but everything is unless homegrown.

Chinese elite have secret organic farms and not for underlings who must eat what WE eat.

$10,000 wasted on clothes to learn to avoid most fabrics because of chemicals that gets IN us.

Spandex rhymes with sex: poisonous clothes called "sexiness"

Decrease total load thru diet then you can wear a little spandex--it's a budget or get sick.

Wearing synthetics is a prison robe cuz it's the worst torture (acid, dizzy, nausea) I've known.

Clarity reflects like a diamond while contradiction is bloated planes/you won't make a mint.

Grand dad lived on bread and butter, died at 90 slender, lustrous and with shiny black hair.

Which is higher: mukbang fame (gluttarians) or fine violin?

Pray, for He can give you life extension, sudden health, saving your spouse or de-age the vessel.

Eat breakfast whether you want it or not then work/fast 24 hours you nut.

LE FEMME and the Communist Spirit

One digestive burn, perfect. Two: horrible. Three: impossible, you'll end up in a hospital.

Why do pies and cakes make you lose weight faster? Cuz starch with fat brings satiety longer.

Skin dryness indicates time to switch.

Brush thy face as you detox while fasting after breakfast.

My Korean cotton came and I'm so happy cool again this stuff is magic and chic, very decent.

If your gut rolls look like the side of the moon you're on the wrong food.

Some gotta indulge their wants to learn why they suk like how ten Big Macs change their looks.

Pot oil cured cancer with two weeks to live, it's the answer. Vitality and rosy cheeks with color.

Hemp oil brought such a sudden cure radical she gave up pharmaceuticals and looked beautiful.

Hemp oil corrects wrongs/makes it all right. Like Donald Trump it's God's answer to blight.

Gluttons suffer demon possession from undigested meals in the intestine and the process of addiction.

Pharmaceuticals distort what God made but hemp oil brings us to it and we look forward to it.

Rosy cheeks and a spring in his step: if that's what he has it's hemp oil we should all get.

IF: Intermittent fasting with 8/16: 8 hours food 16 hours fast and that's it.

With a little load I can't take the petroleum floor. Lesser load thru diet means I can take more.

LE FEMME and the Communist Spirit

I want him to find himself cuz that = good health.

You eat a big dinner/there it sits and you wake up with a big pot feeling in the pits the hedonist blitz.

Debase the west thru chemicals and diet then import pops who look better/never had all that.

Makeup may be vegan but still chemicals--don't think it's innocent just cuz there's no animal.

Put vegan makeup on, feel mildly sick all day. What a joke this is, it's all about chemicals, ok?

I went into a vegan store and smelled chemicals in paint, walls and floor: contradictions/more.

In this billion dollar industry "vegan" just means no animal but not a word about other chemicals.

Everything was so much healthier when including animal cuz now they instead use chemicals.

GMO, soy, corn syrup, canola oil is in everything as main component of fish to fake fruit, you know?

I really got into the rolls and butter then was curious as to why it felt so tight in my sweaters.

After bread and butter I can fast 48 hours: good training/way of justifying.

Gotta have deep roots not just glitter. Fast a little longer then it all drains out and you're lighter.

Fast, now party: shake that bod and wait as the bloat drains out, what a relief not looking so odd.

How to heal now: eat plants you grow and use cannabis oil.

LE FEMME and the Communist Spirit

Why do they have bread and butter for breakfast? So they go 24 hours without hunger-harass.

Pepperoni dog snacks aren't pig but chemicals. Snacks are how they're killing dogs, read labels.

Nice music keeps the pets happy till you get back. Have empathy, they miss you/think about that.

Cheese would be better than fake pepperoni sticks for dogs--gotta be real if you want them long.

My salad inoculated me so I could have a cookie.

You have anorexics and the opposite, bulimics. One eats nothing the other everything in sight.

Just get it in there, don't need a lot just a presence of the superior elements.

SYNTHETIC CREEP

The Nazis are still in charge but rather than taking you to the gas chamber they bring it to you.

Have you seen your synthetic skies? We're controlled by child rapists hellbent on world demise.

Oh oh, spandex and cashmere allergy: for MCS eliminating the best is a test of this new reality.

Everything is spandex, even 5% is too much--it's bad to squeeze in our organs and our lunch.

95% cotton is not enough you must eliminate formaldehyde (the 5% spandex) or you've had it.

When I took all the spandex and cashmere from drawers the room lit up and I was well and floored.

LE FEMME and the Communist Spirit

Cashmere goat is a common allergy which hits those with low immunity, it's hard science reality.

Spandex prevents wrinkles or stretching but the downside is sickening, everlasting, flabbergasting.

Once you've identified spandex allergy you must leave it completely, no elastic in panties.

Most common allergy is to our clothes. At least put em in the garage and feel good again, ya know?

Put all the spandex in garage, repair the damage then take out/wear one at a time perhaps.

The point is to get it out of your environment esp. where you sleep. Sleep is repair, recovery, sweet.

To think I used to sleep in the same room as my wardrobe: a collection of chemicals/microbes.

To walk into their house is a chemical sledgehammer, you're so sick you must escape or a goner.

With empty drawers I can breath again. Just cuz it's contained doesn't mean it's not poison.

If it says 95% cotton we tend to trust it but don't--it's that 5% poison that's gonna bust us.
Spandex is in everything and that's one way they're killing us. It's formaldehyde/death.

I got ill from 5% spandex in my cotton T, I kid you not. Never trivialize importance of 100% or it's rot.

If you have to wear the spandex at least store it in the basement and wear one at a time.

Watch out for "wool blends" cuz that's the same thing, fabric leaven and it'll kill you/you'll hate it.

269

LE FEMME and the Communist Spirit

What touches our skin, what contaminates us most? Our clothes: eliminate saving just a few.

Don't buy used clothes from ebay cuz they have detergents, demons or contaminants unknown.

Develop a spandex allergy and you can't ever have spandex again, it's insidious and lethal man.

Everything is spandex cuz they wanna look sharp in their racing stripes and colors/flamboyance.

I ended up on Icebreaker merino for maximum (less is more) efficiency, clothes close to zero.

Least amount of clothes: maximum adaptation and comfort cooling in heat and warming in cold.

I may wear spandex but don't live with em and sleep fixes it--if beds next to closet forget it.

So you can look slim spandex is your end.

Elastin, lycra, spandex, deadly plastic squeezing in your insides and it's all by plan to kill us.

Synthetic Creep: Icebreaker was 100% wool but now gotta read their labels: lycra, nylon, bull.
Your tee is not 100% cotton--learn to read labels. It's part deadly synthetic making you disabled.

Watch synthetic creep cuz they're sneaking in poison to get close to our skin, that's their way in.

Makes you look thin, squeezes you in. Bright colors, racing stripes and logos from lion's den.

If only 4% of your shirt is poison that's enough to make you nauseous, bloated and noisome.

God said it's too tight and filled with spandex, everything is.

LE FEMME and the Communist Spirit

I love the fit but it makes me sick.

The best athletic smartwool company in the world starts to leak synthetics in and it's sick/foul.

My "smartwool" cami is now 83% wool but 12% nylon and 5% elastin, sickening/lethal poisons.

The company always gives us the good stuff at first but then lets the exterminators in, a curse.

Sample symptoms of synthetics: bloated abdomen, nausea, acid reflux like mad, headache, vertigo.

A smartwool company poisoning those who trust em by leavening nylon/elastin in to kill em.

Poisoned by food, clothes, air, water, people, media and distorted implants for decades back.

The smartwool company actually said nylon made the clothes stronger (tho' we're dead sooner).

But I love the color, style and fit so much I'll try it again but I just know it'll be sickening.

Poisons get in through food and clothes so avoid those but firstly stick to what you know in our Bible.

Icebreaker I love your wool but it's made in China where there are no rules using nylon/elastin too.

Tech fabrics (wrinkle-free, wear resistance, dry fast, water/wind resistant) are lethal synthetics.

Gotta go 100% wool or cotton or poison gets in the door and I've tested it, 5% and I hit the floor.

Can egotist give up bright colors, stripes and shiny fabrics knowing it's killing him? No he can't.

LE FEMME and the Communist Spirit

Loved the fit so thought it's all-ok the 12% nylon 5% elastin cuz 83% is wool and it's longlastin'.

The point is the 10% has mess of chemicals on it so you're still raising the load and will pay for it.

Hard to get 100% cotton or wool there's always a leaven to "strengthen" the fibers or no-wrinklin'.

10% nylon in the blend: First bubbles, then acid, headache, dizziness, abdominal bloat, nausea.

Nylon shorts for men (the athletic kind) cause prostate cancer, impotence and blurred vision.

Thinking it's ok when it's not cuz it's a popular brand they bought. Nylon, spandex, polyester, all rot.

Any lousy factory in China can add 10% synthetic to the mix then you're up a creek/that's all it takes.

Wear 10% synthetic, take drugs for headaches and acid reflux plus depression/anxiety, it sux.

Why is there so much cancer of the sex organs? It's the nylon panties with spandex or elastin.
It's no big thing for them to "strengthen" expensive wool with cheap nylon making it "sexy" ya know.

The athletic "corespun" fabrics mean the nylon's inside of it so just maybe you won't know it.

"We've added a nylon core for extra strength" so now smartwool fabrics makes us sick for life.

It's nothing for them to inject 10% nylon into nice wool--that's "lacing" and it's still poison.

So they only laced it 5% so you say "it's stronger/wrinkle free" then get sick/it happened to me.

LE FEMME and the Communist Spirit

Read your labels and reject athletic fabrics yes they will last forever that's part of the trouble.

Rid of 95% of my wardrobe and feel so good and free. It's the fabrics you see but I need efficiency.

I could see in his pictures pressure building--like a blockhead--ending in an aneurism.

Even cotton is contaminated with spandex, a horrible poison whose only cure is to never have it again.

95% cotton 5% lethal chemical that will kill you.

Shame on companies producing Smartwool now lacing their clothes with poisonous materials.

Rid of spandex etc. outa the house and whole new world opens up: feeling like a kid again, wow.

Synthetics make you sick but are a subtle hex like being depressed/never at your best.

Spandex tube tops: tight spandex around the breasts means cancer and chemically sensitive.

Stop trying to wear synthetics cuz problem isn't going away and you're sick even if under the ray.

Chemical combos are 10x worse than each as one, like the utter illness from polyester with nylon.

Suddenly I'm sick. Fabrics are the biggest surface upon which some kind of chemical sticks.

Young Elvis loved peanutbutter/jelly sandwiches most, that accounts for his great luster and looks.

Starch and butter if you don't have em together you'll be hungry again and have to eat sooner.

LE FEMME and the Communist Spirit

If there's no starvation in the land there's no revolution--they're just too fat and happy. Michael Savage

Wash all new clothes cuz there's diseases from Chinese factories and they've also found feces.

Make tasty healthy cookies and live on those, how easy.

They want us complacent, docile and accepting so it's big pharma that is used to play dirty.

Prescription drugs (Big Pharma) kill more people in America than cocaine, meth and heroin.

Prescription drugs kill 60,000 a year (more than Vietnam) yet CNN was all for these ma'am.

Clean the blinds or it's dust mites.

33% of Americans and 44% of women are obese, unfit, could never defend our great nation one bit.

If donuts fried in butter satiety lasts longer.

Used cashmere, are you kidding? All those threads filled with who knows what/souls unclean.
Get new stuff and wash those/twice should be enough, they sneeze in Chinese factories, huh.

The more complex or nubby the thread the more chemicals and kooties can infest as contaminants.

They have found fecal cells on new clothes.

You can wear it for life and it's so cool. Korean cotton is thick and smooth and indestructible.

Bamboo fabrics give permanent creases, who needs this? Korean cotton cool class: stays nice.

LE FEMME and the Communist Spirit

I felt much better on bread and butter.

Don't keep those clothes around--don't be caught dead in them. it's not who you are, ditch em.

Discard clothes that are for show rather than efficiency cuz you're in the know.

Why do ministers and maestros wear black? They're down to the most basic, the highest in fact.

Not white it shows spots and we're never caught not looking tops.

Suddenly I couldn't wear anything worn by others before, it's a spiritual thing and kooties galore.

When I elected never to wear thrift store items again I felt I had left a dungeon/great elation.

They're all beautiful but have been warn by someone before and it's a spiritual war, no thrift stores.

Weight: As soon as you see a little improvement you know you can go all the way with it.

Like kind: We'll help you out in an emergency but otherwise leave us alone we're busy fasting.

Lady

If women can't hold the line (by the book) but just conform to the norm they become immoral.

Many women have become nasty and dirty--pugnacious, and I don't like em too much.

Most women below fifty are immoral and it's proven by what they vote for like abortion and more.

275

LE FEMME and the Communist Spirit

Most women under 70 are immoral. Few refuse sex before marriage, and there's even more...

Women are immoral by going along with their kids when their job is teaching morality to the twits.

Women are immoral if they forgive without repentance over and over again just creating criminals.

Women under 80 are immoral if they agree to present cultural narratives just to please relatives.

Sure you gotta forgive em but that's for your benefit--doesn't mean you ever have to see em.

I wasn't screaming at you it was my mother hating all men through me cuz I mimicked her until I forgave/was free.

She showed aggression through gossip and exclusions. She put me down but I learned to live without interruptions.

No, she will never let you go cuz she's mad--you know what is said about a woman's wrath.

Men duke it out then become best friends. Women fight thru gossip, reputation-destruction and never talk to em again.

Communist spirit prevails in schools--girls pressured to lend stuff out, be more tolerant or fornicate (be cool).

He's not only bad cuz he's a liar, but cuz he doesn't inspire. Rosie O'Donnell on Donald Trump

I'll scratch you off my list, what an idiot. Thus proving: no lower intellect can ever judge a higher intellect.

Get used to being ignored until that moment you POP into the scene, world.

Don't devolve to attention-getting to compensate for your as-yet-unrecognized genius tho' I know it's frustrating.

LE FEMME and the Communist Spirit

Facebook: banned under vague or nonexistent guidelines. "Hate speech" is whatever *they* don't like or think.

We now must live in the minds of crazy people cuz someone was offended by something we said.

Because they can't manage their own emotions they must control everyone else.

It will never end cuz if you don't manage negative stimuli (snowflake yourself) you become more panicked.

Less and less is required to trigger you more and more and you end up controlling everyone/abhorrent.

On principal we can't demand shut down of liberal outlets engaging in egregious anti-conservative behavior.

Pedophilia and racism do not exist. It's only good vs. evil that causes hell-- what the low people pick.

Total load will go way down now she's not around. Immunity is a budget determining smiles/frowns.

The choice of where you go next is only narrowed by self-doubt.

I'm not into the social part of technology like PHONES. I want to take in infinity and learn it all.

Thank God I'm done so any backlash (to what women are really like) will not degrade the work about jerks.

Of course we hate em they kill their babies and ruin their husbands--that's our brothers, fathers and sons.

Le Femme goes into production tomorrow and I expect an atom bomb of love and relief vs. hate or sorrow.

I'm done with Poli Psych cuz they'll ban me anyway--giving no real guidelines it's just their feeling it's not-ok.

LE FEMME and the Communist Spirit

What keeps coming back are enigmas, contradictions, unanswered questions: blight of smart women.

I see things, or am I seeing things? Help me, please--that's all I said for years on my knees praying to Thee.

Dogs flip into various behavior patterns and humans do too. It can be ferocious so must know the "two".

Death: Ten times more likely over sixty, another ten if you're lucky. Happens fast ya know, so enjoy today.

Poisons get in through food and clothes so avoid those but firstly stick to what you know in our Bible

We took the blame for the whole thing completely forgetting all the slimy things they were doing.

We were brainwashed to support evil.

They hurt me so much and what was it all for, anyway? Years wasted but not really, I worked night and day.

How to get to total world renowned success: never think of em again and that's their karma, man.

So now: Just dress nice then be yourself, stunning.

It's totally trendy to shoot a thousand selfies so I'd go the opposite direction and stay happy.

HOW IT ALL GOES TOGETHER

FEMME

Merkel and Theresa Mae are typical females (I hate to say) but they weren't born that way.

Pathological Altruism: Overconcern for the needs of those who hate you rather than protecting your few.

278

LE FEMME and the Communist Spirit

Women ya got the vote now you're supposed to learn about politics and economics--glassy eyed stare.

No our president doesn't refer to all immigrants as rapists, thieves and murderers but many are.

Women wanna suck off of Big Daddy Government so they won't need men--that was always The Plan.

Along with feminism is the sexual revolution--it is free and a man has many chances to cheat.

Women: stop parading your flesh--you know what I mean cuz women look at women more than men.

Emergent self-protection: Men never meet with a woman now without the door open.

Wimp was asked what's your secret to a long marriage and he said "I just do what she says".

He was a great foil for me. Stark opposites, all his different qualities showed mine by contrast, see?
If one rejects you for your words, then they determine your reality, actions, limits, everything--walk away.

Rejects you for saying something (crossing her lines) but then she comes back, forget her this time.

Say something wrong, lose friend. They come back like nothing happened but censorship/86ed: drop em.

Women: "they're inviolate, you're not allowed to criticize em, I say fuckem'" said man finally done.

What man can live with an articulate woman with the mind of a steel trap? All of em feel daily zapped.

Women should be sweet little ladies. I hate this rough edge: fleshy, shady.

LE FEMME and the Communist Spirit

Don't mess with Jezebel. Men duke it out then become best friends. Women hate forever, no amends.

Women: it's just easier for them to go with the emotional talking points and these facts be damned.

Though a brilliant performer one lost her entire rep in one interview, wrecked.

The minute I walk in church door it's flesh, flesh, flesh everywhere, parading the flesh with flair.

Parading the flesh in front of men--how embarrassing, women! There are lines and you cross em.

If it's that hot just stay home rather than dressing that way/it's ugly.

There were decades of anger as I mimicked my mother.

The women's inability to let people fail means we all get swallowed by disaster. Stefan Molyneux

Most fathers are against the wife/mother who wants to baby murder.

The cries I have heard from the womb have reached my ears like a sonic boom, Lord said in my room.

FRENEMY

Nagging problem: Flaky associates bring constant disappointments so reject this disrespect.

We're nice until we're not then watch out, nuts.

If you're born to do something it's as natural as a bird singing.

You don't go to hell from a bad start but a bad finish. John Hagee

Your unique true self is the raw material God gave you to work with. It's ok to shape/design it/ make it.

LE FEMME and the Communist Spirit

My aristocratic scholarly bloodline stops here--the rest of em are just evil offshoots loving to smear.

Dogs are part of the family so let em be.

Lotsa saved people caught up with the devil: broken lives, broken homes, evil.

It's wives (of men caught with porn) who commit suicide, not the men. Invasion by dark world/alien.

The problem with masochists is when they meet a real sadist.

Be sin free and life becomes perfect too. Don't expect disaster/failure as in the past (just learning tools).

Don't keep remorsing back to lower levels when you didn't know better and filled with demons/fetters.

Possibly a demon for years because of which you acted out, became maudlin or a lush and a louse.

With experience/time you find what works best (FOR YOU) then expand those while deleting the others.

The new cumbaya church music is shallow, emotional, fleshly, sounds the same and is man-centered.

"Quality worship"--from tingle to tingle, search for greater tingle--praise and worship with co-mingle.

All you can do is repent then do what you do best and forget the rest.

Though past doesn't exist it can still make you sick. Forgive yourself for when used by demons, hick.

Things aren't obvious until they are, so be patient and suddenly they'll see afar.

Jesse P. said to treat all thoughts as evil, of the devil--don't trust em but be like cats/dogs, living now.

LE FEMME and the Communist Spirit

Home: A sanctuary in the midst of chaos. Routines of avoidance and fencing in, creating a spiritual/quiet den.

I'm at the tail end of completion of a Creative Act which took a lifetime. Handle carefully, it's so fine!

Don't need marketer. Just be famous for being self--since you've made the books available, they'll sell.

No one makes millions first, you gotta write the book first and it takes years.

Before things are obvious they're not obvious so please, go easy on us. Student

We don't need a book marketer, for example. Just make the books available then God fills the bill.

Of course you're best, 99% of them are half outa their mind and the rest are buffoons, dead in sins, blind.

Ain't no big thing to wait for the bell to ring. Until that ring, nothing. Grace Jones

Style/strength can't be faked. You either have it or you don't yet not thru birth but correcting mistakes.

HIPPY

Go to college with the SJW mob: Come out traumatized with no job.

College traumatized me suddenly. Professors were debauched, hated America, made me think their way.

Trump Derangement Syndrome PART 2: Conservatives feel crazy cuz they lost family over voting this way.

America's coming into it's harvest under Donald Trump, God's anointed. It's payback time: know it.

Obama accused Trump of old political theories as if he were superior destroying America forever.

LE FEMME and the Communist Spirit

Great biographies are fascinating--most died in tragedy after magnificent opulence and notoriety.

We're moving legally from "intent" matters to only "consequences" matter-- legal system is in tatters.

Microaggression: any act that makes the listener uncomfortable regardless of the intent?

Don't trust thoughts, they're of the devil and the past is gone/doesn't exist. Be just here now like dogs/cats.

Only one cure for SJWs and college profs: put em in an Iranian prison to learn about tyranny vs. freedom

Not all ideologies are expressions of psychiatric disorder but many are.

First they ignore you then they laugh at you then they fight you then you win. Gandhi.

The Patriarchy is just western civilization, make no mistake--so they retool us from the bottom up/erased.

If you use language that your ideological adversaries demand you use (gender pronouns) then they've won.
If they can impose linguistic absurdities on you then you've agreed to live the official lie. Don't/stay high.

My highest duty is to restore old paths. God made me this way, at modernists I'm daily pist.

They've so conditioned people to conform that a thinker is totally out of sync and it makes us sick.

Failure to use the proper pronoun (the pronoun that's demanded of you) can result in prosecution.

Journalism or uninformed commentary? One is necessary, the other is tearing down our country.

LE FEMME and the Communist Spirit

When the wicked rule the people mourn. Trump's made us cool though they're tearing him down.

MORAL POSTURING

it's the elevation of moral posturing about sensitivity over truth.

They're making their move--that's why all this evil stuff is happening--so be patient while Trump removes.

They're so concerned about what others think they cripple their own speech.

CNN advocates for "free press" then protests we be censored.

Kids were taken outa normal childhood joys, tracked into sex--robbed of projects/hobbies and hexed.

Heh, God set em up for the kill by tracking em into the virtual world. Maybe we will win, ya know?

How to stop abuse: You take control of the time he spends with--so he can't disappoint, the louse.

Trumps SMV (Sexual Market Value) is just too high as charming/smart billionaire. They can't stand it/gaps too wide.

Trump tells the bloody truth/unthinkingly while Obama gave em a ruse as a big phony/smilingly.

I love freedom. I love America. I love the way things used to be. I'm horrified at the declension, see?

The press isn't the enemy of the people but the fake news (80%) is. Donald Trump

If we show black-on-white crime the media bans us and it's the same in Europe when Islam stabs us.

These people are evil and they're making their move. Alex Jones

LE FEMME and the Communist Spirit

Liberals: 6 x more likely to steal, 9 x less likely to give but 1000 x more like to *say* they're giving.

Children's cartoons are sickeningly vile. Expect devastation cuz God said to protect innocence, n'espa?

When people get weak the first thing they seek is power and there is the devil promising forever.

Major mechanism in the renewal of conservatism is: resurgence of the nation state.

What is liberty? The right to tell people what they don't want to hear and remain totally free.

No logic to a demon other than destruction and your ruination so stop remorsing back and just forget him.

Wash this generation off. It's a gritty smelly dark aura of ugly mauve tones and living with it is very rough.

Can't stand hearing the lies anymore. It's too frustrating and why should I be debased by the whore?

California isn't my country anymore and it won't be until I'm dead--and it makes me sad. John Steinbeck

No black in power has ever been able to help the black community but a white man did who they hated.

Whoever has guns has the power. When it's just government it's not a true democracy and a dire hour.

Trump has been chosen by God to weed corruption. Open borders means one thing: hostile INVASION.

I will clean up the darkness and usher in the light, for I have America in My Hand. The Lord

For Christians praying for impeachment/death of our wonderful God-given president: hell swallows em.

LE FEMME and the Communist Spirit

The smart say democrats will never see the Whitehouse again. This red tsunami is due to their deep sin.

I'm so thrilled at the morality of our president: 15,000 pedophiles arrested yet the news never reports it.

This is the year of major arrests including Hillary/Obama so get ready for catastrophe/social unrest.

About to have the biggest energy explosion in our history. Big companies are moving back, gladly.

Why do they call him a racist when he's the most non-racist president we've ever had? Makes us mad.

Arrogant liberals always talking about their "rights" but what about their wrongs? Disgusting.

97% of news posts on Donald Trump are negative. Due to constitution, we must put up with it.

It's gonna be a red tsunami nationwide so get ready for major arrests of traitors, crooks and pedophiles.

America's set up right now to be the number one producer of ENERGY in 2019.

Initially Trump was to resume his empire after 4 but after seeing the deep corruption it'll be 8 years.

Sorry I had to disappoint my Facebook friends by not posting anymore all cuz of Mark Zuckerberg.

We're outraged after John McCain's glittering funeral turned into a Trump bashing session.

COMMIE

White people were so sweet with their little pets, roses and other plants. Revive our race, save us yet.

LE FEMME and the Communist Spirit

But we're nice to the point of maudlin masochism as we gladly give what is theirs to rapacious invaders.

In the human species it is insanity to care more about out-group than in-group members.

Pros and cons of multiculturalism: One the one hand more beheadings, on the other interesting cuisine.

Multiculturalism: The first bits are interesting then the returns slow down then the problems, profound.

The traveling couple who said evil didn't exist were then killed by ISIS terrorists.

Wherever masses of humans = massive fecal matter but open border liberals don't care about splatter.

Be aware of social impact of stepping over homeless and their feces while exploring the city. Paris Trip Advisory

Poor Germans and their recent guilt complexes apologizing for everything they say and think/stop this.

Confusion is two parallel news universes and that's why it's like we speak two separate languages.

Socialism is philosophy of failure, creed of ignorance, gospel of envy, whose virtue is equal sharing of misery. Winston Churchill

Paris looks more like a bazaar for illegal migrants. Paris trip advisor review

They care more about the extinction of the mold beetle than white people.

Economic migrants become a client group the state controls. Despite murder and rape it's power ya know.

Leaked Soros docs confirm migrant crisis a tool of "global governance". Good grief wake up, liberal dunces.

Swedish rape stats show 80% are foreign born.

LE FEMME and the Communist Spirit

The elites push migrant policies where they're not bearing the brunt of the resulting catastrophes.

The current mode is collective punishment which is the opposite to justice.

Macron agrees Europe needs 200 MILLION migrants in the next 30 years, he's the Kalergi Plan enforcer.

We don't want em here cuz we know MAL-ADAPTATION to insane or loose environments is our.

Tip for hot Paris trip: don't step in the shit.

To repeat. Macron: In the next 30 years 200 MILLION MORE are coming but we have Big Daddy.

Once western culture becomes the minority view you won't have free speech or women's rights ever again.

How do race hustlers get power and wealth? By yelling "racist" that's how.

To find out who rules over you find out who you're not allowed to criticize.

With time the only thing worth talking about can't be talked about.

Signs of radically changed demography: Bags of shit on Frisco sidewalks, bags of body parts in NYC, yuk.

Whites, please have babies. We don't like--we abhor--these cruel brutal cultures with different realities.

They want us all brown, period. One big bag of it easily malleable and accepting of tyranny/used to it.

These people lack empathy and have totally different values when it comes to dear animals/go to hell!

When it comes to animals even the tender mercies of the wicked are cruel.

LE FEMME and the Communist Spirit

They love and enjoy working in meat packing industries. Have you ever wondered why, softies?

While flooded with disparate cultures making us sick all we can do is fence up and live our own trip.

They change the four olds: Old ideas, old culture, old customs and old habits but we don't want this.

We console ourselves in this terrible period by pretending it's not going on.

Thomas Jefferson's version of fake news: the "lies of the day"

Because of Trump, veterans are the new elites. Feminists with comfy existence should just shut up, the creeps.

SELFIX: AUTOPHAGY

Basically I'm on dates—easy, no cook, satiety, sugar for energy, a fruit but dense, see?

There's times I'm into fats like nuts but it's fruit and starches most days just to fill up.

I eat to fill the tank so I can work all day and night but I love to fast, it's outa sight.
Photos make us vulnerable since they're so into looks/critical and we're more into the spiritual (invisible).

It's phony, scary, weird, fake happy, so boring everyone's smiling, say nothing misery camaraderie.

What are they laughing about? It's a phony social glue or veneer smoothing reality with other fakers.

It's always grit on my nerves, hysterical laughing like the cackling of thorns hiding such darkness, forlorned.

Liberalism is a mental illness and if you have to adapt to it (like boss or spouse) you become crazy.

LE FEMME and the Communist Spirit

The fake virtue signaling left are always moralizing yet stand for the lowest evils and debaucheries.

Plants nutritionally dense but not calorically dense so gotta keep eating em--no thanks.

I dreamed of pizzas ex-cheese, French toast w/ butter (much as pleased), decadent buffets, geez. -Vegan

It's just terrible: Anything processed/they're trying to kill us.

Make your own: Potato salad etc. in stores is filled with soybean oil!

Nutritional density means high water and low calories. No, I want satisfaction so I'm not hungry.

I'm down on nutritional density and UP on caloric density for the long haul--high as a kite/having a ball.

People start calling you "old" and you start to decline. Instead, live every moment until you die.

If he always has an eye for a good looking one you know it and life becomes hell/no fun.

Don't get angry, it's the devil. Don't be mad just walk away gently: unhook, block, change info--simple.

It's not the fact you're old but that they'd say it! Ageism is worse than racism but *autophagy will cure it*.

When we don't eat the body eats itself--as inner spaces clear you now have cheekbones/hit on right combo for once.

It's a matter of filling the tank so you can get to work all day with glory to God and it's Him you thank.

The possibilities are endless if you think like this. Just wait, you'll be discovered in fastarian bliss.

LE FEMME and the Communist Spirit

TYRANTS AND PROCRASTINATORS

Tho' enthused at first the flame dies and he goes slow, gets lazy, doesn't know, has no empathy for y'all.

Enthused at first then they flake out. Happy to promise/plan then becomes cold, zombie, a different man.

No staying power, weak foundation, limp handshake, vacillates--that's the immature man/THIRD RATE.

He always thinks he can do it, explosive acceptance--but then distracted by whatever catches his glance.

If they know how important it is to you that's precisely when they'll withdraw/withhold giving it.

Progressives caught in a "purity spiral" of demanding more and more strict adherence to their bull.

Author's note: Forgiving without repentance means they keep doing it. Retire from the tension of dealing with un-empathic fools: do whatever you can to transcend the world.

100 KAREN KELLOCK BOOKS

AFFINITY OR MISERY
AGELESS CORNUCOPIA
AMERICA AWAKE!
AMERICA'S DAFT ERA
ARTS OF PALEO FASTING
AUTOPHAGY ON CHEATERS
BACKSTABBING NEUROTICS
BETRAYAL TRAUMA
BOOMERS AND BROKENNESS
BOOT ON NECK
CHAMPION GUIDES
COMMIE NUTHOUSE
COMMIES
COMMUNIST SPIRIT
CONTAGION OF MADNESS
CONTAGIOUS MADNESS
CULTURE CLASH BASHED
DAFT LEFT
DAILY FASTARIAN
DAM RATS
DIVERSITY IS CRUELTY
E-RACE WHITE
EVIL FREAKS (Beyond Gross)
THE END OR A BEND?
FEMALE BULLIES AND FEMI-NAZIS
FEMALE CARNALITY
FEMALE DUMB DOWN
FEMALE POWER DRIVE
FEMINISM AND RUIN 1 & 2
FIX FOR MISFITS
FOOLS & TRAMPS
FREEDOM SPEAKING
FRENEMY ENABLER
FRENEMY LIAR
FRENEMY THIEF
FRENEMY TRAITOR
TRENEMY TYRANT
GENIUS IS HELD DOWN
GLOBALISLAM
GOD USES THE FLAWED
HAZE OF THE LATTER DAYS

THE HERD IN WORDS
HIX POLITIX
HOW THEY RUINED US
JUST SKIP DINNER
LE FEMME AND THE COMMUNIST SPIRIT
LIBERAL CHAOS & ROT
LIBERAL DOUBLETHINK
LIBERAL GALL 1 & 2
LIBERAL SHOVE-DOWNS
LOCK YOUR GATE
LOSERS and Femme Fatales
MANUAL FOR SUPERIOR MEN
MODERN ART FROM HELL
MOSTLY FAKE
NOTES TO CHAMPS 1 & 2
OVERCOME FRENEMIES
PC MAKES US CRAZY
PEOPLE ARE CRUEL
PEOPLE PROBLEMS 1 & 2
PERSECUTED GENIUIS
POLI-PSYCH MYSTERIES
PRETENTIOUS SLOBS
QUEEN BEE
RED NEW DEAL
RETURNING TO FIRST NATURE
SEASON OF TREASON
SEPARATE MEANS HOLY
SOCIAL HYPNOTISM
SOLITUDE SOLUTION
SUPERCILIOUS
THE SCHOOLS SCREWED EM UP
TOAD TO PRINCE
TRIALS CYCLES
TRUMP VS. GROUP
TRUST IN TRASH
THE TRUTH ABOUT PEOPLE
UNDERHEANDEDLY CLEVER
WALK TALL WITHIN WALLS
WE'RE NOT ALL ONE
WINNERS SKIP DINNER
WORK OR SMERK

293

AUTHOR BIO
Karen Kellock Ph.D.

Ph.D Political Psychology, UCI 1976
Post-Doctoral: UCI Medical School
Department of Psychiatry
Grants NIMH, NIAAA

Ph.D. dissertation "A Systems-Theoretic View of Pathologic Interaction" made an early mark as the "Wife of the Alcoholic Syndrome". Postdoctoral research at UCI Medical, Dept. of Psychiatry on the systems surrounding pathology on NIMH and NIAAA federal grants: *The Contagion of Madness: The Psychology of Neurotic Interaction and Pathological Systems*. Therapy tool Therapeutic Playwriting introduced the play *Mary and Murv: Gruesome Twosomes in the Alcoholic Marriage*. She taught Abnormal Psychology and Pathological Systems Theory at UC and CSU campuses and developed "the Debris Theory of Disease" in five books and website: (www.karenkellock.org): *Champion Guides, Daily Fastarian, Just Skip Dinner, Arts of Paleo Fasting, Ageless Cornucopia. Manual for Superior Men is a* pick-it-up-anywhere book that you can't put down (20,000 Kellockialisms) and ever on your desktop it should be found (or this Ebook for superior wordsearch of new jargon).

www.ingramcontent.com/pod-product-compliance
Lightning Source LLC
Chambersburg PA
CBHW061003280326
41935CB00009B/815